PRAISE FOR INNOVATI
FAST TRACK

Innovation is rapidly becoming the critical success factor of the twenty-first century. To survive and thrive in the modern business environment requires companies to think differently, to implement breakthrough ideas with rigour and to stand out from their competition – in short to innovate. Innovation Fast Track *provides the necessary insights, challenge and solutions to:*

→ *identify critical gaps in your current innovation performance*

→ *implement an integrated approach to innovation from ideas to implementation, and*

→ *develop the leadership skills you need to succeed in this key role.*

Lindsay Brook, HR Director, Nokia

FAST TRACK TO SUCCESS

INNOVATION

FT Prentice Hall

FINANCIAL TIMES

In an increasingly competitive world, we believe it's quality of thinking that gives you the edge – an idea that opens new doors, a technique that solves a problem or an insight that simply makes sense of it all. The more you know, the smarter and faster you can go.

That's why we work with the best minds in business and finance to bring cutting-edge thinking and best learning practice to a global market.

Under a range of leading imprints, including *Financial Times Prentice Hall*, we create world-class print publications and electronic products bringing our readers knowledge, skills and understanding, which can be applied whether studying or at work.

To find out more about Pearson Education publications or tell us about the books you'd like to find, you can visit us at **www.pearsoned.co.uk**

FAST TRACK TO SUCCESS

INNOVATION

ANDY BRUCE AND DAVID BIRCHALL

An imprint of **Pearson Education**

Harlow, England • London • New York • Boston • San Francisco • Toronto • Sydney • Singapore • Hong Kong
Tokyo • Seoul • Taipei • New Delhi • Cape Town • Madrid • Mexico City • Amsterdam • Munich • Paris • Milan

PEARSON EDUCATION LIMITED

Edinburgh Gate
Harlow CM20 2JE
Tel: +44 (0)1279 623623
Fax: +44 (0)1279 431059
Website: www.pearsoned.co.uk

First published in Great Britain in 2009

ISBN: 978-0-273-71988-5

British Library Cataloguing-in-Publication Data
A catalogue record for this book is available from the British Library

Library of Congress Cataloging-in-Publication Data
Bruce, Andy.
  Fast track to success innovation / Andy Bruce and David Birchall.
     p. cm.
  Includes bibliographical references and index.
  ISBN 978-0-273-71988-5 (pbk. : alk. paper) 1. Technological innovations--Management.
  I. Birchall, D. W. (David W.) II. Title.
  HD45.B737 2009
  658.4'063--dc22
                                2008053789

The publisher is grateful for permission to reproduce the tables on pages 18 and 160–3. These items are reproduced by permission of Derry, S., 2008, Project Leaders International.

10 9 8 7 6 5 4 3 2 1
13 12 11 10 09

Typeset in 10/15 Swis Lt by 30
Printed by Ashford Colour Press Ltd., Gosport

The publisher's policy is to use paper manufactured from sustainable forests.

CONTENTS

The Fast Track way ix

About the authors xii

A word of thanks from the authors xiv

Innovation Fast Track xvi

How to use this book xx

Fast-Track-Me.com xxi

A AWARENESS 1

1   Innovation in a nutshell 5

2   Innovation audit 17

B BUSINESS FAST TRACK 29

3   Fast Track top ten 33

4   Technologies 61

5   Implementing change 79

C CAREER FAST TRACK 93

6   The first ten weeks 97

7   Leading the team 115

8   Getting to the top 139

D DIRECTOR'S TOOLKIT 155

T1   Team innovation audit 159

T2   Integrated innovation framework 165

T3   Market and competitor scanning 169

T4   Creativity techniques 177

T5   Innovation project checklist 181

The Fast Track way 187

Other titles in the Fast Track series 189

Glossary 190

Index 199

THE FAST TRACK WAY

Everything you need to accelerate your career

The best way to fast track your career as a manager is to fast track the contribution you and your team make to your organisation and for your team to be successful in as public a way as possible. That's what the Fast Track series is about. The Fast Track manager delivers against performance expectations, is personally highly effective and efficient, develops the full potential of their team, is recognised as a key opinion leader in the business, and ultimately progresses up the organisation ahead of their peers.

You will benefit from the books in the Fast Track series whether you are an ambitious first-time team leader or a more experienced manager who is keen to develop further over the next few years. You may be a specialist aiming to master every aspect of your chosen discipline or function, or simply be trying to broaden your awareness of other key management disciplines and skills. In either case, you will have the motivation to critically review yourself and your team using the tools and techniques presented in this book, as well as the time to stop, think and act on areas you identify for improvement.

Do you know what you need to know and do to make a real difference to your performance at work, your contribution to your company and your blossoming career? For most of us, the honest answer is 'Not really, no'. It's not surprising then that most of us never reach our full potential. The innovative Fast Track series gives you exactly what you need to speed up your progress and become a high performance manager in all the areas of the business that matter. Fast Track is not just another 'How to' series. Books on selling tell you how to win sales but not how to move from salesperson to sales manager. Project management software enables you to plan detailed tasks but doesn't improve the quality of your project management thinking and business performance. A marketing book tells you about the principles of marketing but not how to lead a team of marketers. It's not enough.

Specially designed features in the Fast Track books will help you to see what you need to know and to develop the skills you need to be successful. They give you:

→ the information required for you to shine in your chosen function or skill – particularly in the Fast Track top ten;

→ practical advice in the form of Quick Tips and answers to FAQs from people who have been there before you and succeeded;

→ state of the art best practice as explained by today's academics and industry experts in specially written Expert Voices;

→ case stories and examples of what works and, perhaps more importantly, what doesn't work;

→ comprehensive tools for accelerating the effectiveness and performance of your team;

→ a framework that helps you to develop your career as well as produce terrific results.

Fast Track is a resource of business thinking, approaches and techniques presented in a variety of ways – in short, a complete performance support environment. It enables managers to build careers from their first tentative steps into management all the way up to becoming a business director – accelerating the performance of their team and their career. When you use the Fast Track approach with your team it provides a common business language and structure, based on best business practice. You will benefit from the book whether or not others in the organisation adopt the same practices; indeed if they don't, it will give you an edge over them. Each Fast Track book blends hard practical advice from expert practitioners with insights and the latest thinking from experts from leading business schools.

The Fast Track approach will be valuable to team leaders and managers from all industry sectors and functional areas. It is for ambitious people who have already acquired some team leadership skills and have realised just how much more there is to know.

If you want to progress further you will be directed towards additional learning and development resources via an interactive Fast Track website, **www.Fast-Track-Me.com**. For many, these books therefore become the first step in a journey of continuous development. So, the Fast Track approach gives you everything you need to accelerate your career, offering you the opportunity to develop your knowledge and skills, improve your team's performance, benefit your organisation's progress towards its aims and light the fuse under your true career potential.

ABOUT THE AUTHORS

ANDY BRUCE is widely acclaimed as an authority in innovation management – covering the creative and innovation process from ideas to implementation. He has worked with corporate and public sector clients over the last 15 years to help improve performance and profitability through the introduction of what he refers to as an integrated innovation framework.

In the late 1990s, Andy founded two companies specialising in innovation and project management. The first, SofTools,[1] develops web-based applications to enable management visibility, control and confidence over their pipeline of new ideas and their portfolio of implementation projects. The second, Project Leaders International,[2] provides consulting and training services to assist the adoption of innovation and project management best practices.

Andy previously worked as a management consultant, focusing on the design and implementation of organisational change. Clients included corporates such as EDS, Nokia and Coca-Cola, as well as public service organisations such as the Department for Work and Pensions, the Ministry of Defence, Trust hospitals and even political parties.

Before working as a consultant, he served a short service commission with the Army, (Royal Electrical and Mechanical Engineers) and worked in a variety of engineering and commercial roles for a manufacturer of computer-driven production machinery – his last two years as a company director working on market research projects in Australia.

Andy gained a BSc at Southampton University in 1981 and an MBA at the Australian Graduate School of Management in 1990. He is also currently Programme Director of the International Business Accelerator programme at Henley Business School.

[1]SofTools: www.SofTools.net
[2]Project Leaders International: www.Project-Leaders.net

He has written a total of eight business books, including the best-selling *Strategic Thinking* and *Project Management* titles in the Dorling Kindersley Essential Manager series.

Andy Bruce, SofTools,
Greenlands, Henley-on-Thames, Oxfordshire, RG9 3AU, UK
E Andy.Bruce@SofTools.net
T 00 44 (0) 1491 412 400
W www.SofTools.net

DAVID BIRCHALL is a Professor at Henley Business School and has developed innovative management programmes, and researched and advised organisations on innovation performance. He has worked on projects in many European countries and spoken extensively at conferences in the US and Asia. With George Tovstiga, David co-authored *Capabilities for Strategic Advantage: Leading Through Technological Innovation*. His current research focuses on capabilities in business building.

E David.Birchall@henley.reading.ac.uk

A WORD OF THANKS
FROM THE AUTHORS

We would like to thank the following for their generous contributions to this book.

→ **Liz Gooster, Pearson.** There are many exciting new ideas in the publishing world at present, but without an enthusiastic champion, most will simply die a slow death. Liz had the confidence to commission the Fast Track series and associated web-tool on behalf of the Pearson Group at a time when other publishers were cutting back on non-core activities. She has remained committed to its success – providing direction, challenge and encouragement as and when required.

→ **Ken Langdon.** As well as being a leading author in his own right, Ken has worked with all the Fast Track authors to bring a degree of rigour and consistency to the series. As each book has developed, he has been a driving force behind the scenes, pulling the detailed content for each title together in the background – working with an equal measure of enthusiasm and patience!

→ **Mollie Dickenson.** Mollie has a background in publishing and works as a research manager at Henley Business School, and has been a supporter of the project from its inception. She has provided constant encouragement and challenge, and is, as always, an absolute delight to work with.

→ **Critical readers.** As the Fast Track series evolved, it was vital that we received constant challenge and input from other experts and from critical readers.

→ **Professor David Birchall.** David has worked to identify and source Expert Voice contributions from international academic and business experts in each Fast Track title. David is co-author of the Fast Track *Innovation* book and a leading academic author in his own right, and has spent much of the last 20 years heading up the research programme at Henley Business School – one of the world's top ten business schools.

Our expert team

Last but not least, we are grateful for the contributions made by experts from around the world in each of the Fast Track titles.

EXPERT	TOPIC	BUSINESS SCHOOL/ COMPANY
Professor Ben Dankbaar	Designing innovative organisations (p. 14)	Nijmegen School of Management (NSM), The Netherlands
Professor Julian Birkinshaw	Building a better organisation (p. 25)	London Business School
Professor George Tovstiga	Capturing return on innovation – the learning bit (p. 58)	Henley Business School, University of Reading
Professor Klas Eric Soderquist	Open innovation (p. 76)	Athens University of Economics and Business, Greece
Professor David Birchall	Innovation in services (p. 90)	Henley Business School, University of Reading
Professor Ben Dankbaar	Global sourcing and Innovation (p. 112)	Nijmegen School of Management (NSM), The Netherlands
Dr Rebecca Steliaros	The sourcing of new knowledge for strategy making – tapping into the best brains (p. 135)	Engineering and Physical Sciences Research Council, Swindon
Associate Professor Josiena Gotzsch	Innovation through design (p. 152)	Grenoble Ecole de Management, France

INNOVATION FAST TRACK

*Innovation is probably the hottest topic of today, but why?
Most industries are now highly competitive, with better-
informed customers expecting 'more, faster, cheaper and
better' all at the same time. Few companies can compete
purely on price and so most now have to differentiate to
survive, and to differentiate you must innovate.*

Innovation may be the hottest topic in business today, but whilst everybody talks about it and agrees that it is important, there is no one
general roadmap to success. So how do you turn innovation from a marketing concept into something tangible with an impact on the bottom
line? There is of course no simple answer, and to succeed a different
way of thinking and working is required – one that combines analytic
and creative thinking and that focuses as much on implementation as it
does on ideation.

Practical innovation is therefore a key concern for many businesses.
Increasing global competition over the last five years has brought grow-
ing pressures. Western businesses can't make their products cheaper
than the so-called BRICK countries (Brazil, Russia, India, China and
Korea), so what can they do to differentiate themselves from the flood of
companies targeting their markets from overseas? The developing
countries are hungry, eager and internet-enabled and pose a major
threat, but these expanding markets also present many opportunities for
expansion for companies willing to think differently and innovate.
Companies in every country and all industry sectors must innovate to
survive, let alone thrive.

But for innovation to be more than a buzzword it has to be deeply
embedded into a business's structure. It was experiences with small
entrepreneurial businesses and large corporates, including Nokia and
Coca-Cola, that led us to develop a model for integrated innovation
management. Whilst these market leaders are not necessarily seen as
the most creative companies, both Nokia and Coca-Cola have taken a

sustainable approach to innovation involving every member of staff actively seeking out new opportunities and new and better ways of doing things.

As you seek to implement your approach to innovation, one caveat is important: don't expect every attempt at innovation to succeed. Most of the top global companies have had notable failures – think of Coca-Cola and their UK launch of Dasani, or Dyson's attempt to move into washing machines. They're not necessarily failures of innovation. Nine times out of ten, the reason innovation ideas fail is because those involved haven't thought through the potential pitfalls and 'what could go wrong'. Often the likely reasons for the failure aren't difficult to spot – a consumer focus group could do it – but, historically, the people in charge of innovation are enthusiastic positive thinkers and don't want to look at the negative side.

We are going to talk about the **six Ps** that companies that innovate successfully tend to get right: planning, pipeline, process, platform, people and performance (see figure). All are elements of an integrated framework – like a chain, it's only as strong as the weakest link.

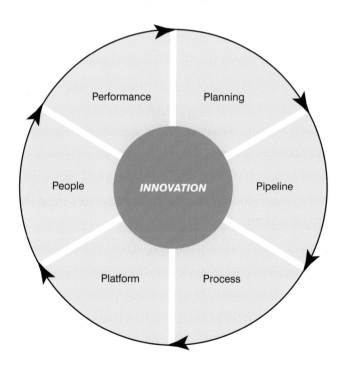

Taking the six Ps in order, **planning** reflects the fact that innovation needs to start with strategy. Over the next few years, what are the high-growth or high-revenue areas the CEO wants the company to focus on? What success factors will you need to consider when planning something new? For a fizzy drinks supplier, for example, an obvious strategic driver would be the trend towards health drinks. Planning therefore provides a context or focus for innovation activities, enabling ideas to be generated that address critical business issues.

It isn't, of course, enough just to have an idea. A **pipeline** reflects the fact that ideas must be captured, organised, screened, prioritised and managed. Unfortunately this is often determined by who shouts the loudest or which senior manager has a pet idea. That's not how you want to choose. Without a structured pipeline, people become disillusioned as they watch the organisation follow the wrong ideas.

Process is about managing creative ideas through to implementation – what is often called project management in other areas of business. Everybody likes to have a good idea, but somebody has to take it from the generic concept through to successful implementation. This includes everything from assessing the idea's feasibility and creating a detailed business case, to developing, piloting and implementing it – and, after rollout, helping to feed back good experience into further future ideas or lessons on how not to do it.

Platform refers to web-based software that tracks an idea from its time in the pipeline to assessing its value post-implementation. It is not just a task and resource-planning tool; it gives senior managers visibility, control and confidence over the entire innovation portfolio. The software also ensures that all teams follow a common approach based on best practice, and provides the status reports needed at the regular review meetings.

An effective innovation framework also needs the commitment of key stakeholders: **people**. Senior managers need to be open to new ideas, as innovation thrives only in a supportive culture. There needs to be a champion who drives every idea through to completion, and an executive sponsor who allocates the necessary budget, time and resources, and motivates the team. And at all levels of the organisation people are effectively the eyes and ears of the business, constantly scanning for market trends and competitor activity.

We like to cite Nokia as a leader in the area of innovation. Mike Butler, then Managing Director of the Nokia UK Product Creation Centre, set only two ground rules for the 18 people who took part in an innovation workshop: 'No ideas around time travel or teletransportation – have fun!'. He then walked out leaving the team to get on with it. Out of that initial workshop came ideas that now, ten years later, are helping convert Nokia from simple mobile handsets to complex lifestyle communications devices (see the Case Story on p. 6). Current new services such as making credit card payments via mobile phones and downloading music or games on to phones were ideas on the table in that workshop ten years ago.

Performance, the final P, drives all of this. The critical success factor for integrating and introducing innovation is how you monitor performance – defining the key innovation performance indicators, agreeing who sits in the monthly review meeting and focusing the agenda on innovation. Too often, today's managers are too fixated by the company's profit and loss statements, the information that impresses actual or prospective shareholders. But financial reports tend to focus on past performance, which we liken to trying to drive a car by looking in the rear-view mirror. Whilst keeping an eye on the current financials is important, future success depends on getting your plan for innovation right and implementing it effectively in order to keep your organisation that one step ahead.

Innovation needs champions, people who will drive through the problems and setbacks, convince sceptics of the need to do new things and make a good idea produce results. Perhaps you are that champion: perhaps just for your team or division of the company, or perhaps for the entire organisation as the Chief Innovation Officer. If so you have an exciting time ahead. Remember, once a great idea is recorded it can never die; but there's a lot to get right before you can be sure that it will fly: so let's get on with it.

HOW TO USE THIS BOOK

Fast Track books present a collection of the latest tools, techniques and advice to help build your team and your career. Use this table to plan your route through the book.

PART	OVERVIEW
About the authors	A brief overview of the authors, their background and their contact details
A **Awareness**	*This first part gives you an opportunity to gain a quick overview of the topic and to reflect on your current effectiveness*
1 *Innovation in a nutshell*	A brief overview of innovation and a series of frequently asked questions to bring you up to speed quickly
2 *Innovation audit*	Simple checklists to help identify strengths and weaknesses in your team and your capabilities
B **Business Fast Track**	*Part B provides tools and techniques that may form part of the innovation framework for you and your team*
3 *Fast Track top ten*	Ten tools and techniques used to help you implement a sustainable approach to innovation based on the latest best practice
4 *Technologies*	A review of the latest information technologies used to improve effectiveness and efficiency of innovation activities
5 *Implementing change*	A detailed checklist to identify gaps and to plan the changes necessary to implement your innovation framework
C **Career Fast Track**	*Part C focuses on you, your leadership qualities and what it takes to get to the top*
6 *The first ten weeks*	Recommended activities when starting a new role in innovation, together with a checklist of useful facts to know
7 *Leading the team*	Managing change, building your team and deciding your leadership style
8 *Getting to the top*	Becoming an innovation professional, getting promoted and becoming a director – what does it take?
D **Director's toolkit**	*The final part provides more advanced tools and techniques based on industry best practice*
Toolkit	Advanced tools and techniques used by senior managers
Glossary	Glossary of terms

FAST-TRACK-ME.COM

Throughout this book you will be encouraged to make use of the companion site: **www.Fast-Track-Me.com**. This is a custom-designed, highly interactive online resource that addresses the needs of the busy manager by providing access to ideas and methods that will improve individual and team performance quickly. Top features include:

→ **Health Checks.** Self-audit checklists allowing evaluation of you and your team against industry criteria. You will be able to identify areas of concern and plan for their resolution using a personal 'Get-2-Green' action plan.

→ **The Knowledge Cube.** The K-Cube is a two-dimensional matrix presenting Fast Track features from all topics in a consistent and easy-to-use way – providing ideas, tools and techniques in a single place, anytime, anywhere. This is a great way to delve in and out of business topics quickly.

→ **The Online Coach.** The Online Coach is a toolkit of fully interactive business templates in MS Word format that allow Fast-Track-Me.com users to explore specific business methods (strategy, ideas, projects etc.) and learn from concepts, case examples and other resources according to your preferred learning style.

→ **Business Glossary.** The Fast Track Business Glossary provides a comprehensive list of key words associated with each title in the Fast Track series, together with a plain English definition – helping you to cut through business jargon.

The website can also help answer some of the vital questions managers are asking themselves today (see figure overleaf).

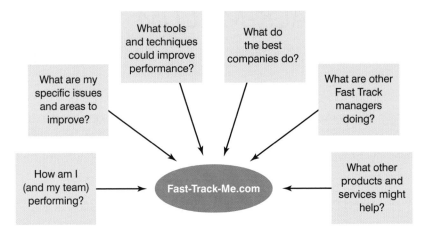

Don't get left behind: log on to **www.Fast-Track-Me.com** now to get your career on the fast track.

AWARENESS

This book introduces a sustainable approach to innovation aimed at keeping you, your team and your organisation at the forefront of the process, thus contributing towards the future of all three. The starting point is to gain a quick understanding of what innovation is and what it is not, and to be aware of your own and your team's capabilities in this area right now. For this reason we will ask you a number of questions that will reveal where you and your team need to improve if you are truly to have a culture of and meet the aims of innovation – an exciting product set for your customers and business processes that will put your service to customers amongst the leaders in your industry.

'Know yourself' was the motto above the doorway of the Oracle at Delphi and is a wise thought. It means that you must do an open and honest self-audit as you start on the process of setting up your framework for innovation.

The stakes are high. Innovation is at the heart of success in this global, competitive marketplace. Your team, therefore, need to be effective innovators and you need to be a good leader in innovation. Poor leadership and poor team effectiveness will make failure likely. An effective team poorly led will sap the team's energy and lead in the long term to failure through their leaving for a better environment or becoming less effective through lack of motivation. Leading an ineffective team well does not prevent the obvious conclusion that an ineffective team will not thrive. So, looking at the figure below, how do you make sure that you and your team are in the top right-hand box – an innovative and effective team with an excellent leader? That's what this book is about, and this section shows you how to discover your and your team's starting point.

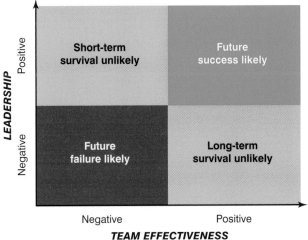

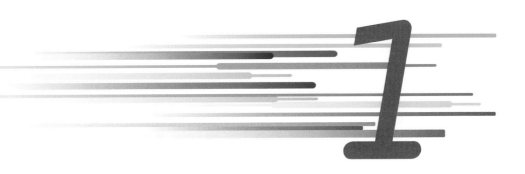

INNOVATION IN A NUTSHELL

Starting with the basics

Just what is innovation?

Some people think that innovation is simply the generation of new ideas, but we would refer to this as creativity. New ideas are worth nothing if no one takes those ideas forward and puts them into practice. When people implement new ideas we can call that innovation. Innovation in business terms then becomes 'the commercial exploitation of ideas'. So you and your team not only need to generate ideas that will improve your performance but also have to do something about them. This can be very difficult, particularly if the new idea steps on the toes of some of the beliefs and processes of the organisation that have been in place for a long time.

So to truly become an innovative team you have to effectively combine the phase when you generate creative ideas, thinking outside the box if you like, with a structured and rational screening and implementation process so that a successful change will bring improved results.

Why is it so important?

Innovation is not a new concept but it is certainly getting a lot of attention in the current business landscape, so we have to ask ourselves – why?

Fifteen years ago, organisations could survive on the basis of a good product if it was kept up to date with tweaks and changes to maintain competitiveness and give opportunities for marketing relaunches, the so-called mid-life kicker.

 CASE STORY **NOKIA PRODUCT CREATION, MIKE'S STORY**

Narrator Mike led the development of Nokia's new mobile phone products for the Japanese and American markets at a time when the company was driving for global leadership.

Context In the late 1990s Nokia was the number-three mobile phone business in the world with aspirations of leapfrogging Motorola and Ericsson to become global leader. It had grown quickly on the back of a rapidly expanding technology-driven market.

Issue However, the future of the telecoms industry would be driven less by technology than by lifestyle in the coming years. Functions would remain important, but brand and user experience would have an increasing impact on purchasing choices. Furthermore, technologies were merging and global partnerships with other product and technology providers would be required. This changed competitive landscape required a new approach and a different way of thinking.

Solution Mike decided to initiate a series of cross-functional innovation workshops where he wanted to encourage people to think differently. He introduced the first event simply by setting a couple of boundaries, 'I don't want you to consider tele-transportation or time-travel – have fun!', at which point he walked out.

Learning This short but motivational speech set the culture perfectly, and two days later the team had generated 120 ideas, of which they would take the top 20 further over the coming months. This new process and mindset helped Nokia achieve its goal of global leadership within a three-year period.

Over the last 15 years, however, three major trends have emerged:

1 **Maintaining competitiveness has become a relentless drive towards improved efficiency and effectiveness.** Just think of the things that cost relatively or even actually less than they did 15 years ago: clothes, electronic goods, white goods, toys… and we could go on. And the consumer is getting a better product with better after-sales service. The drive therefore to improve

service and reduce costs has led to changes in how organisations go about their tasks. Project management is becoming a core business tool – so that companies can deliver what they say they are going to deliver, on time and within budget. Most organisations are experimenting with and applying continuous improvement techniques such as total quality management, Six Sigma, lean, theory of constraints and so on.

2 **Companies face increasing expectations from their customers and consumers.** Customers have got used to continuous improvement in what the business world offers them. They are better informed about possibilities because of access to information – in part fuelled by the internet, which offers opportunities for product/price comparisons that were impossible in the days when the only way you could get that information was from biased advertisements and walking round the shops. Put simply, customers want more for less, and they want it faster. They won't accept mediocrity because if we can't deliver, someone else will.

3 **Globalisation: no matter how big or small you are, you are now competing in a global market.** The corner shop, struggling with higher prices because it lacks the buying muscle of the big boys, is now also competing head to head with sellers on eBay, and with a national retailer offering home-delivery.

Gary Hamel[1] summed this up as: 'Those that live by the sword will be shot by those that don't!' Our summary is that if you can't compete on the basis of price you have to differentiate – and to differentiate, you have to innovate!

QUICK TIP BUSINESS ENVIRONMENT
Constant monitoring of your business environment will help to identify significant ideas for change (opportunities and threats). Look for trends and ask, 'So what? How will this impact me or my team?'

---

[1] Hamel, Gary (2002), *Leading the Revolution*, Boston MA: Harvard Business School Press.

So why is it difficult – what typically goes wrong?

So, recognising how important innovation is to the future success of a company, let's start by looking at what can go wrong. This should make you think about particular areas in your business or team where one or more of these problems occur and focus your attention on fixing them.

1 **The team leader, founder or chief executive is not open to ideas.** This can have a very negative impact on the team in two ways. Firstly, it can stifle creative thought; after all if the boss isn't open to new ideas then what is the point of coming up with any? Secondly, even if plenty of new ideas are identified, a reluctance to share them with others means that they will simply not go anywhere.

2 **There are too many 'sacred cows'.** Even when the senior team are enthusiastic about innovation in general, there are often specific areas where discussion is curtailed. These might relate to personal hobbyhorses, areas where someone has had a bad experience previously, something that is too complicated for a key person to get their head round or even a perceived personal threat to a person's position or standing in the business. Ideas are met with sweeping statements ('We don't sell in Europe'; 'We are not in frozen produce') that curtail discussions in areas that may in fact be critical to future success.

QUICK TIP CHANGED AGENDA
Put innovation on the agenda at your regular team meetings and stimulate group discussion by asking questions that challenge current thinking.

3 **Nobody cares – there is no perception of the need for innovation or a reward mechanism for the innovators.** Even if the chairman's statement in the annual report talks about the importance of innovation, unless this is translated into tangible actions that reflect day-to-day activities, and unless people are rewarded for great ideas, then people on the whole won't

bother. It is not that they don't care; it is just that most people are too busy dealing with other priorities. Lack of innovation stores up problems for the future because you're too busy dealing with the pressing problems of today.

4 **There is no guidance on the boundaries to innovative ideas.** This decreases confidence. Whilst the idea of setting boundaries for any creativity session is counterintuitive (we're supposed to be creative, aren't we?), without boundaries two things are likely to happen. The first is that the ideas are less likely to be aligned to current business goals, and will therefore probably not happen – this can be very demotivating to the person with the idea. Secondly, participants don't tend to take it so seriously if there is no clear focus point or context – rather like turning up to a meeting where there is no agenda.

5 **There is no structure or method – so the wrong ideas are generated or prioritised.** Brainstorming alone is rarely sufficient to generate the right creative ideas. Innovation workshops need to have a clear purpose and structured agenda. By all means include creativity tools and techniques, but use them within a broader innovation process that impacts how all teams within the company operate all the time. The lack of a clear process for taking ideas from concept to completion will lower the overall probability of success.

6 **Logistics get in the way – poor facilities, equipment or an inexpert facilitator.** Imagine locking a team of five people in a small room with grey walls and no external windows on a hot day, and then asking them to come up with new creative ideas. Choice of venue, timing and space, as well as the use of a trained facilitator, can make a dramatic difference to the quality of ideas generated.

7 **Not enough time is allowed.** All too often people are too busy to stop and think, let alone be creative. As individuals we may be too reactive – responding to one email or crisis. In a group situation lack of time tends to make the team focus on analysis of the first few ideas rather than exploring some of the more obscure ideas that may come out later on and prove to be the winners.

8 **Inability to implement.** Nothing can come of ideas if they do not get new money and resources allocated to their implementation, and all too often really great ideas come to nothing. If we don't have a plan that expects changes to occur, we must expect others to allocate insufficient resources or time or budget. This results in ideas that fail to deliver, and it can also kill off a culture of innovation simply because people won't see the point of producing a good plan for change when they know there will be no resources to implement it.

QUICK TIP TIME AND BUDGET
Work to a time frame and budget, as this will focus the internal team and build a reputation for delivering.

---

9 **Innovation is not seen as a priority.** Innovation is only a priority if the CEO regularly reviews it. Even given the right resources, people will not see innovation as a priority in the business, and it will quickly die if the senior managers do not review the topic regularly.

10 **Innovation is seen as another fad.** For many 'innovation' is just seen as the latest management fad. 'The boss has just been on another workshop, or read another book.' There is no real belief in the team that anything will actually change, and if it does, it probably won't be sustainable.

These potential pitfalls can be addressed in isolation, or as part of an integrated framework as presented in the Director's Toolkit in Part D.

So just what is innovation? – frequently asked questions

The following table[2] provides quick answers to some of the most frequently asked questions about the topic of innovation. Use this as a way of gaining a quick overview.

---

[2] All features throughout the book are available on the companion website: www.Fast-Track-Me.com

FAQ 1 What is innovation?	**1**	Innovation can best be described as the commercial exploitation of ideas. This implies that innovation will need to combine creative thought with the ability to implement successfully. Ideas must also encompass all aspects of business performance improvement – not just products and services.
FAQ 2 Why is innovation important to our business when profits and revenues are good?	**2**	The pace of change in business today is phenomenal. What is profitable and successful today may be out of date or copied by competitors tomorrow. Innovation is the key to differentiation, and differentiation is the key to staying ahead.
FAQ 3 What types of innovation are there?	**3**	Generically there are: product/service innovation (new or upgraded products or services); process innovation (new ways of producing, sourcing or manufacturing); market innovation (new markets or new ways of delivering goods and services); and business innovation (business transformation, business model innovation and diversification).
FAQ 4 Who should be involved in the innovation process?	**4**	Everyone! If you can create a culture of innovation where it is part of the DNA of your business, then you stand a better chance of becoming more and more successful. You may start with a few 'innovation primers' around the business, but innovation is not the exclusive preserve of marketing or R&D.
FAQ 5 Surely the point about innovation is that it occurs when someone has an idea – you can't plan for it, can you?	**5**	It may seem an oxymoron but the most innovative companies are those that plan innovation into their business cycle. Focused innovation workshops, on a relevant theme, can held be quarterly. Innovation planning can be incorporated into the annual business plan and an ideas board can generate ideas daily.
FAQ 6 Are creative people born or made?	**6**	Both! It's what you do with an idea that is important. Even mundane or dry ideas can get results. Some people may come up with more ideas and more inspired ideas than others, but getting everyone involved in innovation, to whatever degree, is still the best way forward.
FAQ 7 How does innovation link to long-term success?	**7**	Continuously improving what you are doing today may not be enough for long-term survival, let alone success. If your industry is changing rapidly, then only improving dramatically on an existing product or breaking into a new market can set you apart from competitors.

FAQ 8 Where do the best ideas come from?

8 Anywhere. Therefore you need an innovation process that captures ideas from customers, suppliers, staff, social trends, academia and formal research. Don't forget mistakes. Plenty of the best product innovations were accidents: Post-its, Superglue and Champagne to name but three!

FAQ 9 How can we make ideas visible across the business?

9 Most companies, no matter how small, have access to the internet or have an intranet of some sort. It makes sense to distribute ideas across the company to show what is being done and to spark further spin-off ideas. The days of the white-board in the corridor are numbered.

FAQ 10 What are the pitfalls of a suggestion scheme?

10 Suggestion schemes can often die a very quick death. If you ask for ideas and then don't reply quickly enough, explaining the reasons why ideas have been rejected, you run the risk of killing off any further ideas from staff. Suggestions also tend to be individually based, and schemes therefore have to be managed and constantly improved. A suggestion scheme may be worthwhile, but it is rarely the starting point and will only ever be one small part of an integrated approach to innovation.

FAQ 11 What is the best way of filtering out bad ideas?

11 Having a set of objective criteria against which all ideas will be measured, in advance, is the *only* way of filtering out poorer ideas (no such thing as a 'bad' idea). Make sure everyone knows what these criteria are and why you have them, ahead of their submissions. However, make sure you test your criteria thoroughly as you don't want to kill off ideas simply because they are unusual, and if you think you are rejecting good ideas then review the criteria, as they should not be set in stone for eternity.

FAQ 12 Is innovation relevant to service companies and the public sector?

12 Absolutely. Everyone thinks innovation is synonymous with products and product development, but in today's service economy innovation is equally valid to service companies. Think of new ways of providing your services as well as the services you provide.

FAQ 13 What amount of innovation is appropriate?

13 The amount spent on innovation should reflect the goals set by the business senior team, which in turn will reflect business performance. If there are ambitious growth targets or a critical need to turn business performance around, innovation spend must go up. If the business is highly profitable and in a steady state then the need for innovation is less. However, few organisations can ever be accused of spending too much.

FAQ 14 *How do I measure the cost and return on innovation?*

14 Using standard project management tools and techniques, you can easily do a return on innovation investment (ROII) calculation. Consider the impact on profitability or business goals, and the associated costs in terms of resources consumed during implementation. Recognise that calculations will not be easy and there will be uncertainty in your measurements.

FAQ 15 *How do I know if my innovation process is working?*

15 Setting your innovation objectives in advance is crucial to assessing whether your innovation management process is working. Are you measuring success by the number of new products launched or by the number of ideas going before your review panel? Check what other companies are doing and how you compare. At the end of the day, business key performance indicators that are showing improvement are the most relevant measures.

FAQ 16 *What are the risks of not being innovative?*

16 Without innovation companies stop changing. This is OK in static markets, but few organisations operate under such conditions. For most it is also not possible to complete on cost alone, and so to survive organisations need to differentiate, and to differentiate they need to innovate. You do not want to be the most efficient producer of what you do today if nobody wants it tomorrow.

FAQ 17 *Will focusing on innovation take my eye off operational priorities?*

17 Historically, good operational teams have always had one eye on continuous process improvement. A structured approach to innovation takes this concept further and pushes the ideas that all departments should constantly strive to improve products, services, routes to market, processes, etc. through formal innovation processes.

FAQ 18 *How much of the budget should I allocate to innovation activities?*

18 It depends on your business and the goals you have set for your innovation programme. Some technology and research-based companies spend a very high proportion of their revenue on R&D and innovation. Try to do a return on investment (ROI) calculation of the value of new products, services and markets to your company and invest as much as you can afford. The key is to make sure investment in tomorrow's ideas is in today's budget.

FAQ 19 *What skills are required to be innovative?*

19 It seems that the most innovative individuals and companies value certain attributes rather than definitive skills: attributes such as 'open-mindedness' and 'flexibility'. The tenacity to see things through to a definitive conclusion is often highly valued. However, effective teams will also have a range and balance of skills.

FAQ 20 *Is innovation a fad?*	**20** Innovation in all its forms is central to successful business. The most successful companies since the Industrial Revolution have been those bringing in new ideas to market before competitors. Call it what you will, innovation is the *key* management skill for the twenty-first Century.

QUICK TIP INNOVATION FATIGUE

Plan the launch of new products and services carefully, as innovation fatigue may turn people off.

We hope that these FAQs give a quick start to getting to grips with innovation. The rest of this book shows you how to move from understanding what the key elements of innovation are to an active implementation of innovation either within your team or division, or company-wide if that is your role.

Designing innovative organisations

Professor Ben Dankbaar[3]

One of the earliest books to appear under the title *The Management of Innovation* was written more than 40 years ago by Burns and Stalker.[4] Not surprisingly, it does not deal with all the issues and techniques discussed in handbooks on the same subject today. It does not contain discussions of research and development, stage-gate processes, multi-disciplinary teams, project management and all the other practices associated with modern innovation management. Instead, it deals with the relationship between organisations and their environment. For Burns and Stalker, management of innovation was concerned with survival in a turbulent environment. Basically, they argued that if changes are frequent and unpredictable, the organisation needs to be structured in such a way that it can react quickly and creatively to whatever comes up. In their empirical

[3] Dankbaar, B. (ed) (2003), *Innovation Management in the Knowledge Economy*, London: Imperial College Press.
[4] Burns, T. and Stalker, G.M. (1961), *The Management of Innovation*, London: Tavistock.

work, they had found that organisations operating in a changing environment had what they called 'organic' structures, characterised by loosely defined tasks and responsibilities, horizontal rather than vertical communication and considerable latitude for employees to guide and direct their own work. These structural characteristics enabled organisations to react and adapt to challenges in the environment.

More recent studies tend to define innovation management in a more proactive fashion. Innovation management today involves the implementation of strategies for the more or less continuous renewal of the product portfolio of companies and of the underlying production processes. This is more than reacting to changes in the environment; it also aims actively to change and indeed create the environment in which the firm wants to survive. Are the insights offered by Burns and Stalker still useful today? Later research has shown that successful innovative organisations are not necessarily characterised by loosely defined tasks and responsibilities and other features identified by Burns and Stalker. And indeed, these features seem to be more appropriate for small organisations or for research laboratories than for big corporations. But the comparison of organisations with organisms is still useful to understand the design requirements for innovative organisations. Burns and Stalker showed that the traditional 'mechanistic' design of organisatons was inadequate in a rapidly changing environment. They argued that organisations had to be perceived as open systems, just like organisms that survive in constant interaction (breathing, digesting) with their environment.

Being organic, then, implies the ability to perceive disturbances, changes and chances in the environment and to act upon these perceptions in a timely fashion. Over the past 40 years, researchers have uncovered various ways in which companies can be organic in this particular sense. We now know that innovative organisations have to incorporate the following elements:

1 a decentralised system for the generation and identification of ideas for new and improved products and processes, including ideas coming from outside the organisation;

2 a well-structured system for the selection and further development (or sale) of the most promising ideas, including a set of criteria based on a long-term vision for the company;

3 efficient structures for the production and delivery of (new and existing) products and services;

4 a well-organised system to register feedback from customers and react to it.

INNOVATION AUDIT

In order to improve performance you first need to understand what your starting point is, what your strengths and weaknesses are and how each will promote or limit what you can achieve. There are two levels of awareness you need to have. The first is to understand what the most successful innovative teams or businesses look like, how they behave and how near your team is to emulating them. The second is to understand what it takes to lead such a team – do you personally have the necessary attributes for success?

QUICK TIP CREATIVE THINKING
Make sure you add creative thinking to your selection criteria when recruiting people to join your team.

Team assessment[1]

Is my team maximising its potential to innovate?

Use the following checklist[2] to assess the current state of your team, considering each element in turn. Use a simple Red-Amber-Green evaluation, where Red reflects areas where you disagree strongly with the

---

[1] You can complete your self-audit and team audit online at the companion site: www.Fast-Track-Me.com.
[2] Table on p. 18 from Integrated Innovation Framework, Project Leaders International, 2008: www.project-leaders.net/innovation-management.php. Reprinted with permission.

statement and suggests there are significant issues requiring immediate attention, Amber suggests areas of concern and risk, and Green suggests everything is good and needs no immediate attention.

ID	CATEGORY	EVALUATION CRITERIA	STATUS
Innovation			RAG
1	Leadership	Innovation is a strategic priority: it is owned by a member of the senior executive team and its importance has been cascaded down through all management levels	☐
2	Strategic focus	Senior management have defined the extent and direction of innovation, there is an external customer focus across the organisation and there is an integrated approach to innovation	☐
3	Internal sources of ideas	Sufficient time and budget is allocated to the internal generation of ideas that focus on achieving performance breakthroughs, and ideas are captured in a central database	☐
4	External challenge	Trends in the industry are monitored, key competitors are understood and there is a systematic scanning (researching) process to keep market insights up to date	☐
5	Idea evaluation	Ideas are formally screened against agreed criteria to ensure they are aligned to business goals and there is an integrated process from idea to implementation	☐
6	Projects and implementation	Implementation initiatives follow best practice project management principles, have sufficient resources and budget, and address issues and risks	☐
7	Support systems	There is a common web-based tool that provides visibility and control over the ideas portfolio, ensures teams follow a common process and encourages continuous learning	☐
8	Innovation champions	Innovation champions exist in all teams across the business, their roles are formally defined and they have the necessary time and skills	☐
9	Creative culture	There is a culture of creative challenge and innovation where mistakes are accepted and people are motivated to engage in innovation activities	☐
10	Performance management	There are agreed key performance indicators for the innovation framework, a clear process for review and a culture of learning and improvement	☐

QUICK TIP *LEARN FROM MISTAKES*
Mistakes can be a great source of ideas and innovations. Review rejected ideas and previous failures and never ever throw the idea away completely.

Having identified where the gaps are in your business or team capabilities, you need to understand if you are the right person to be leading the team as an innovation champion.

QUICK TIP *ONLINE SUPPORT*
Log on to **www.Fast-Track-Me.com** and do your innovation audit online.

Self assessment

Do I have what it takes?

This section presents a self-assessment checklist of the factors that make a successful Fast Track leader in innovation. These reflect the knowledge, competencies, attitudes and behaviours required to get to the top, irrespective of your current level of seniority. Take control of your career, behave professionally and reflect on your personal vision for the next five years. This creates a framework for action throughout the rest of the book.

Use the checklist overleaf to identify where you personally need to gain knowledge or skills. Fill it in honestly and then get someone who knows you well, your boss or a key member of your team, to go over it with you. Be willing to change your assessment if people give you insights into yourself that you had not taken into account.

Use the following scoring process:

0 Not yet recognised as a required area of knowledge or skill

1 You are aware of the area but have low knowledge and lack skills

2 An area where you are reasonably competent and working on improvement

3 An area where you have a satisfactory level of knowledge and skills

4 An area where you are consistently well above average

5 You are recognised as a key figure in this area of knowledge and skills throughout the business

Reflect on the lowest scores and identify those areas that are critical to success. Flag these as status Red, requiring immediate attention. Then identify those areas that you are concerned about and flag those as status Amber, implying areas of development that need to be monitored closely.

ID	CATEGORY	EVALUATION CRITERIA	SCORE	STATUS
	Knowledge		0–5	RAG
K1	Industry and markets	Knowledge of your industry sector in terms of scope (boundaries), overall size and growth, and major trends. This should include an understanding of natural segmentation of products and markets	☐	☐
K2	Customers and competitors	Information about major customers, in terms of who they are and their must-haves and wants. Also an understanding of who the best competitors are and what they do, plus supply chain options and capabilities	☐	☐
K3	Products and services	An understanding of current products and services and how they perform in the marketplace against the industry leaders. This should include substitutes or solutions available from companies in different industries	☐	☐
K4	Business drivers	Insights into current and emerging technologies, legislation, environmental and economic trends that will impact on future product design, access to market or process improvements	☐	☐

ID	CATEGORY	EVALUATION CRITERIA	SCORE	STATUS
	Competencies		0–5	RAG
C1	Creative thinking	Ability to use various techniques to challenge the current state and identify new product, market and process improvement breakthroughs	☐	☐
C2	Root cause analysis	Ability to appraise a situation and analyse factors that could enable or cause a dramatic improvement in performance	☐	☐
C3	Project management	Ability to define, plan, monitor and control change activities in order to deliver identified performance improvements on time and within budget	☐	☐
C4	Risk management	Ability to think ahead and identify, prioritise and mitigate barriers to effective and enduring implementations of ideas	☐	☐
	Attitudes			
A1	Positive approach	Belief that you can make a difference and get things done. Avoidance of looking like a victim of circumstances when you have to overcome resistance from other people	☐	☐
A2	Seeking synergies	Willingness to look for ways to creatively combine several ideas (even if they are other people's) in order to develop a new and exciting concept	☐	☐
A3	Inquisitive mindset	Awareness of the need to constantly seek more effective or efficient ways of doing things. Willingness to challenge the status quo and ask why things are as they are	☐	☐
A4	Breakthrough thinking	Not accepting average or second best. Constantly seeking ways to dramatically change the way things are	☐	☐

ID	CATEGORY	EVALUATION CRITERIA	SCORE	STATUS
Behaviours			0–5	RAG
B1	Determination and commitment	Being prepared to see things through. Although no project goes according to plan, you are not put off by early setbacks or problems – you are resilient	☐	☐
B2	Visible and active support	Making it clear that you are supportive of priority ideas in the way you allocate your time, resources and budgets	☐	☐
B3	Encouraging others	Enthusiastic in coaching and mentoring others who have ideas or who are involved in the implementation of ideas. Looking for ways in which you can be the catalyst for the team	☐	☐
B4	Positive challenge	Challenging the ideas of others in a positive way, helping them to think differently about the way things are	☐	☐

QUICK TIP OPEN TO IDEAS

Ask members of your team how open they think you are to new ideas.

CASE STORY DOWNER EDI MINING, SHANE'S STORY

Narrator Shane (senior partner of Mainsheet – Australia's leading strategy consulting firm[3]) assisted Downer to radically reduce operating costs in a competitive commodity-driven market.

Context Downer EDi Mining is one of Australia's largest and most successful mining companies. It has been successfully delivering open-cut and underground mining services for more than 80 years, and the company has a long track record in both coal and metalliferous mining.

[3] www.mainsheet.com.au

Issue Like many companies in this sector, Downer was hit by reductions in raw material and commodity prices globally and by the spiralling costs of transportation. However, the company had a history of continuous improvement and an enviable reputation for the effectiveness and efficiency of its operations.

Solution A new way of thinking was required. Firstly, it used the services of an experienced consulting firm in this sector (Mainsheet Corporation) to identify opportunities across all aspects of its supply chain – effectively buying in ideas from outside the business. Secondly, with Shane's help, it implemented a web-based tracking tool to provide visibility, control and ultimately confidence over its improvement initiatives.

Learning The company recognised that there is a limit to how much innovation can be driven from inside the business and that often it requires an outside stimulus to take the innovation programme to the next level. However, ideas alone are not enough – success also requires a mechanism and discipline to see ideas through to their conclusion.

Learning

Take a few minutes to reflect on the leadership–team effectiveness matrix overleaf and consider your current position: where are you and what are the implications?

→ **Bottom left – poor leadership and an ineffective team.** This will result in failure. Who knows, you may already be too late.

→ **Top left – great leadership but a poor team.** You have a great vision but will be unlikely to implement it, and so it will have little impact. You will need to find a way of developing and motivating the team and introducing systems and processes to improve team effectiveness.

→ **Bottom right – poor leadership but a great team.** You are highly effective and efficient as a team but may well be going in the wrong direction. It is no use being the most innovative and efficient developers of black and white televisions if there is no market!

→ **Top right – clear leadership and direction combined with an efficient and effective team.** This is where we want to be. Lots of great new ideas for innovation linked to current business goals and with a team unit capable of delivering on time and within budget. You don't need this book; please give it to someone else!

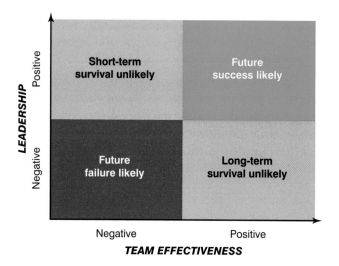

TEAM EFFECTIVENESS

STOP – THINK – ACT

Part A has given you a quick overview of what innovation is, and you will also have assessed the performance of yourself and your team against best-practice checklists. This will have raised your awareness of what is possible and clarified where you are now. Take time to reflect on your profile in order to:

1 identify any 'quick wins' you could achieve today;

2 use the rest of the book effectively.

Look for areas where you could get a 'quick win' and improve matters in the short term. Ask yourself and the team these questions:

What should we do?	What will we change today and what difference will it make (why)? How will we know if it has been successful?
Who do we need to involve?	Who else needs to be involved to make it work and why?
What resources will we require?	What information, facilities, materials, equipment or budget will be required and are they available?
What is the timing?	When will this change be implemented – is there a deadline?

Visit **www.Fast-Track-Me.com** to use the Fast Track online planning tool.

 ## *Building a better organisation*
Professor Julian Birkinshaw

If you were to start a new company tomorrow, what proportion of your time would you allocate to developing and selling a unique product? And what proportion would you devote to building a distinctive organisation? If you are like the vast majority of entrepreneurs, you would focus on the product. The product is your source of revenue. The product is what makes you distinctive. The product is what investors want to hear about. Issues of management and organisation are entirely secondary – they get attention only when they become obstacles to selling more products.

So is it possible for an entrepreneur to succeed by developing a unique internal organisation first, and worrying about the product second? Yes it is. Consider the case of Henry Stewart, founder of Happy Computers. In the early 1990s Stewart was, by his own admission, a stressed-out, small businessman. He had cut his entrepreneurial teeth on the launch of the *News on Sunday*, a radical, left-wing newspaper. The group behind it had no business background but managed to raise £6.5 million. It was lost in six weeks.

'That's where I learned the importance of good management,' Henry Stewart reflects. 'It was a great irony that a company set up on humanistic principles was the worst place to work. There was endless backbiting, meetings, no clear decision making, and endless blame. And so after that, and the experience of getting sacked from my next job, I decided I didn't want to work for anyone else again. I would work for myself and work at how you create a great place to work, how you deliver great service, while being effective and principled.'

With an IT background and an affinity for people, Stewart homed in on IT training as his niche, and set out to build a great IT training company based on a distinctive set of management principles. Principle number one was that managers need to get out of the way to let people perform – they should be coaches and coordinators, not in-your-face managers. 'If you get into work and have a message that your manager wants to see you at 2 pm – do you feel excited?' asks Henry Stewart. 'The most radical thing we believe is that managers should be chosen according to how good they are at managing people. They are usually chosen for technical competence and how long they've been in the job. As a result, one of the biggest reasons people leave a company is to get away from their manager.'

A second key area was recruitment. 'One of the things that really gets me is that most recruiting is absolutely terrible,' says Stewart. 'In my presentations I put up a big picture of David Beckham and a big picture of John Motson and ask which one would your company recruit using the standard recruitment procedure? Most people recruit the one who's good at talking about it, not the one who's good at doing it.'

Happy never asks for qualifications – it is 'profoundly discriminating' and the qualifications requested usually have no relation to the job. Happy does not advertise: it has details of 2,000 people waiting on its website with their email addresses. When a vacancy occurs they are emailed and asked two questions: why do you want to work for Happy and what makes a great trainer? And rather than use an interview, Happy takes prospective employees through a condensed two-hour training module. 'We're looking for people who are supportive of each other, and people who have the potential to train others. So we ask them to prepare a 15-minute session, and then to see how they cope with change we tell them they've got to do it in six minutes. They deliver their session. And then we coach them and they deliver it again. We are looking to see an improvement over the first round. If they deliver the same session they don't get in.'

Happy has ten distinctive management principles (**www.happy-people.co.uk/manage**), including 'Celebrate mistakes' and 'Peer appraisal for managers'. And the results speak for themselves: Happy's staff turnover is around 9 per cent, less than half the industry average. It has never lost a member of staff to a competitor. And customer satisfaction is 98.7 per cent.

Remember, clients often view IT training as a commodity – as a tedious necessity, rather than an important service. But Happy runs courses at £200 a day while its biggest competitor sells them at £90 a day. And while the industry has contracted by 30 per cent over the last six years, Happy's turnover has doubled – without any advertising. 'Our basic philosophy of marketing is to deliver great service and wait for the phone to ring,' laughs Henry Stewart. 'Most companies understand what the customer wants, but most companies then put in place a system of processes and rules that prevent their frontline staff from delivering it.'

There is an important underlying message here. You don't necessarily need a unique product to succeed. Happy sells IT training, just like hundreds of other companies. What makes it different is the attitudes, skills and engagement of its staff – and these qualities are an outgrowth of the company's distinctive management principles, not its positioning in the marketplace. So if you are an entrepreneur, the message is: build a better organisation – and the world will beat a path to your door.

PART B

BUSINESS FAST TRACK

Irrespective of your chosen function or discipline, look around at the successful managers whom you know and admire. We call these people Fast Track managers, people who have the knowledge and skills to perform well and Fast Track their careers. Notice how they excel at three things:

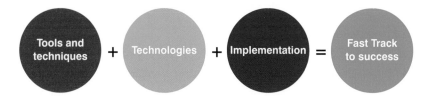

Tools and techniques

They have a good understanding of best practices for their particular field. This is in the form of methods and techniques that translate knowledge into decisions, insights and actions. They understand what the best companies do and have an ability to interpret what is relevant for their own businesses. The processes they use are generally simple to explain and form a logical step-by-step approach to solving a problem or capturing data and insights. They also encourage creativity – Fast Track managers do not follow a process slavishly where they know they are filling in the boxes rather than looking for insights on how to improve performance. This combination of method and creativity produces the optimum solutions.

They also have a clear understanding of what is important to know and what is simply noise. They either know this information or have it at their fingertips as and when they require it. They also have effective filtering mechanisms so that they don't get overloaded with extraneous information. The level of detail required varies dramatically from one situation to another – the small entrepreneur will work a lot more on the knowledge they have and in gaining facts from quick conversations with experts, whereas a large corporate may employ teams of analysts and research companies. Frequently when a team is going through any process they uncover the need for further data.

Technologies

However, having the facts and understanding best practice will achieve little unless they are built into the systems that people use on a day-to-day basis. Fast Track managers are good at assessing the relevance of new information technologies and adopting the appropriate ones in order to maximise both effectiveness and efficiency.

Implementation

Finally, having designed the framework that is appropriate to them and their team, Fast Track managers have strong influencing skills and are also great at leading the implementation effort, putting in place the changes necessary to build and sustain the performance of the team.

How tightly or loosely you use the various tools and techniques presented in Part B will vary, and will to a certain extent depend on personal style. As you read through the following three chapters, first seek to understand how each could impact you and your team, and then decide what level of change may be appropriate given your starting point, authority and career aspirations.

FAST TRACK TOP TEN

This chapter presents a framework of methods or techniques to improve performance and make life as an innovating team easier. Each function can take a lifetime to master, but the Fast Track manager will know which areas to focus on – get those areas right and the team will perform. Often success relates to the introduction of simple tools and techniques to improve effectiveness and efficiency.

Introducing innovation tools and techniques

What needs to be included? – the top ten tools and techniques

Within the area of innovation, the 'top ten' tools and techniques are reflected in what are often referred to as the six Ps of an integrated innovation framework.

Planning will set the overall innovation strategy and will include leadership (specifically the visible and active commitment from the top down) and strategic focus (the identification of high growth and high emphasis products and markets):

1 Leadership

2 Strategic focus

Pipeline covers the development of the list of innovative ideas with activities such as scanning (external and competitor monitoring) and open innovation (developing networks and relationships):

3 Internal sources

4 External sources (scanning and open innovation)

Process introduces a structured approach to the evaluation of ideas (including the initial capture, screening and prioritisation) and a formal 'gating' process for planning and tracking from ideas to implementation:

5 Idea pipeline evaluation (capture, screening and prioritisation)

6 Project and portfolio management (planning and tracking from ideas to implementation)

Platform covers the use of support systems to provide a level of visibility, control and confidence:

7 Support systems

People focuses on the personal side that is critical to success, including appointing innovation champions and developing a blame-free culture:

8 Innovation champions (and virtual teams)

9 Creative culture (blame free, challenging creativity)

Performance emphasises meeting innovation key performance indicators (KPIs) and the operation of the innovation review board:

10 Performance management (the innovation review board)

 CASE STORY **MACPHIE, RONNIE'S STORY**

Narrator Ronnie leads Macphie's sales and marketing activities and was responsible for the initiation of an innovation programme that moved beyond new product development.

Context Macphie is a leading manufacturer of food ingredient products for the European bakery and food services markets. It is a family business and has an enviable reputation for quality and flexibility of service.

Issue As the food industry continued to consolidate, Macphie found it was competing with larger and larger companies who were reducing their supply chain costs through economies of scale. This, together with volatile raw material input costs, meant that Macphie could be at a significant disadvantage on the basis of cost, and therefore had to differentiate – and to differentiate it had to innovate.

Solution Working with outside advisers, Ronnie and others at Macphie reviewed the common success factors adopted by industry leaders and developed an integrated innovation framework specific to its needs. Implementation started by putting the suggestion scheme on hold and then defining the strategic framework and the specific business imperatives for the current year.

Learning By aligning innovation activities across the organisation to business success factors, the number of ideas did not increase, but the relevance and value went up considerably. Ideas were more likely to get approval, funding and management focus, and as a result the enthusiasm for the innovation programme gathered momentum from across all teams.

1 PLANNING *Leadership*

Experience indicates that one of the most important factors in creating an innovation culture is having leaders and teams with ability and commitment. Senior managers need to understand the strategic direction and how innovation can help. They also need to enthuse others to concentrate on current priorities.

Get commitment from the senior management team and your boss to a culture of continuous innovation. It is a 'must' – a necessary prerequisite for success – that senior people lead the way. This must be more than a one-off statement and should be a visible ongoing commitment. It also requires agents of innovation and innovation teams across the organisation, champions who will assist a project manager with the implementation and tracking of ideas, innovations and changes.

Organisations that invest in their people and understand the value of their ideas ensure that facilities, equipment, time and resources are available to help foster ideas and innovations. They use facilitators to help identify new ideas in business meetings, set aside 'quiet areas' for people to think through ideas, and hold informal 'coffee breaks' where people in different departments, who would not normally meet, get together for a break and to chat about ideas.

There are thousands of ways in which staff and management can do things differently and be encouraged to voice their ideas. Where this runs contrary to the way in which organisations are run and jobs designed, it is a key responsibility of managers to 'audit' the organisation in terms of how 'friendly' it is towards being innovative and then to put in place actions to address concerns.

The senior team also needs to clarify and communicate the specific business needs that will drive innovation activities in the current year. Without a thorough understanding of the current priorities, the organisation risks investing a lot of time and money in activities and initiatives that have minimal impact on performance. The key is to connect your innovation to the strategic plan of your division and your organisation as a whole. The task is to make sure that your innovative thinking is concentrating on current business imperatives, sometimes called key success factors. Find these out from the annual business planning process or a strategy session that involves the board, or from managers two levels above yourself.

Once you have identified these imperatives, you can make sure that you align all aspects of innovation to these current business priorities. Also as part of the preparation to innovate, translate the list of imperatives into clear innovation key performance indicators so that you are clear what you are aiming to achieve and when. For example, if there is a key imperative for the organisation to increase its business in a particular market area, identify the target for growth. When you then come to thinking creatively about how to make changes, you will be focused on what it is vital to achieve.

In order that new product development is driving towards high emphasis and high growth areas, you must identify what these are. Similarly, operational innovations should aim to create sleeker supply chain processes to deliver future products to future markets. All this implies that, armed with the right information, you will be able to adopt a more proactive approach to innovation based around innovation work-shops that focus on business priorities as opposed to free-for-all suggestion schemes.

2 PLANNING *Strategic focus*

Successful managers link core business processes to their planning processes, and innovation is no exception. Separating innovation from business strategy diverts key resources and damages the focus of an organisation: avoid this 'missile looking for a target' syndrome.

You determine the extent and type of innovation by examining business performance and by assessing your organisation's tolerance to risk. There are essentially three types of innovation strategy, illustrated below. Those organisations operating in the green areas in the figure can probably innovate with their existing resources and skills. They're doing no more than focusing new product ideas on extending the existing range of products. For example, a vacuum cleaner manufacturer that produces 28 variants of its existing design and technology is carrying out a product modification strategy; it will probably not need new technology or skills to implement this, but it is a very limited form of innovation.

MARKETS AND CUSTOMERS

		Current	Extended	New
PRODUCTS AND SERVICES	Current	Process improvement	Market development	**New capabilities**
	Modified	Product development	**New capabilities**	**New business development**
	New	**New capabilities**	**New business development**	**Strategic change**

Even for organisations wishing to pursue a consolidation strategy (current products in current markets), innovation can be focused on process improvement work. In the green area businesses can operate quite successfully, however businesses cannot continuously improve during times of crisis. In situations where businesses must address a key issue or 'crisis', new capabilities and resources are necessary (orange, central areas in the matrix). A company breaking into a new market (say Japan) with its current product range might need to acquire new manufacturing or sales capabilities.

Truly innovative strategies, the red areas in the bottom right-hand corner, throw up higher risk – because products and/or markets are new to the business. This will necessitate the acquisition of new resources, capabilities, ideas and possibly even leadership. These are commonly called diversification strategies. A strategic change in the business might even require a new business model, and the mergers and acquisitions or licensing routes may be the best way to go.

The extent of innovation is also dependent upon your business's appetite for risk and its current risk profile. Different types of innovation project have different risks. A balanced innovation portfolio includes a balance of risk factors so that some are higher risk with higher return and others are at the opposite end of the spectrum. There is a clear need to assess and manage the optimum number of ideas or innovations at any one time.

There are also different ways in which new ideas will be implemented, and perhaps a useful classification is to identify which are strategic-change projects, as opposed to those that can be managed as business-as-usual, and those that will be managed internally rather than through a partnership or spin-out approach.

3 PIPELINE OF IDEAS *Internal sources*

Once your organisation has accepted innovation as a concept planned at strategic level, you have to address the practical implications of an innovation process or system. An effective starting point is to understand where innovations originate and how to collect and screen them.

Innovations and ideas come from any part of an organisation. They can result from planned activities (such as focused innovation workshops) or reactive on-the-spot ideas stemming from discussions with customers or suppliers. Internal brainstorming sessions focused on a particular business issue are sometimes referred to as 'skunk works',[1] and they can result in highly innovative ideas for performance improvement, assuming that you have involved the right people and created the right environment.

Idea generation is also not the preserve of the R&D or marketing department. Nor is it merely limited to an employee or customer 'suggestion scheme'. Market and customer insight (MCI) can originate from anyone or any team that has eyes and ears, and this in turn can stimulate ideas for improvement from anyone who has time to stop and think. Wherever they originate, it is important to collect, coordinate and manage new ideas as a source of valuable information that is vital to the future of an innovative business. Many successful companies operate an 'innovation war room' where all ideas and innovations are collected and coordinated.

Some organisations will adopt a more proactive approach to the generation of new ideas and will link it into the formal planning cycles of the business at three levels:

1 **The annual business planning (ABP) process.** The natural outcome of a strategic review of the business, typically occurring once a year, is a number of change projects – many requiring a high degree of challenge and innovative thought. These projects often reflect current business imperatives and need to be implemented at some point during the year.

2 **Structured or 'themed' focused innovation workshops (FIWs).** These are formal planned workshops designed to address specific issues. Issues typically include the list of business imperatives where the objective of each FIW is to identify innovative ways of improving performance in each imperative. However, these workshops could also be pulled together at short notice, and whilst they are still structured, they will be in response to a crisis or opportunity that has occurred unexpectedly in the

[1] Popularised by Tom Peters (2004), *In Search of Excellence*, London: Profile Business.

market – such as the merger of two competitors. Each work-shop should be facilitated, be focused on a current business imperative and follow a structured agenda from creative thinking to analysis and action planning.

3 **Ad hoc day-to-day activities.** This reflects the ideas occurring whilst people in all functions carry out their daily routines. The key is to ensure that the current priorities of the business are communicated effectively and that there is an effective method for capturing and prioritising the ideas for action.

QUICK TIP **INDUSTRY LEADER**
Make sure that one member of your team is constantly watching the industry leader and the rising stars – who are they, what are they doing and why?

Some of the routines, such as the annual business planning process and focused innovation workshops, are 'proactive' by nature – a conscious focus on bringing ideas and concepts forward into the innovation process. Some ideas will be more 'reactive' in response to a particular event, and where the culture encourages innovation discovery. Remember that it is market and customer insights that typically stimulate and drive innovation. For the FIWs to work effectively, make sure that each is fed by specific MCIs (see figure). Whatever the situation, the use of trained facilitators can dramatically impact both the quantity and quality of the new ideas for performance improvement.

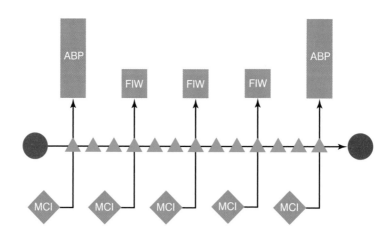

Very innovative companies also develop an 'internal ideas market' culture. Managers have established budgets for innovations and get together to fund the implementation of ideas, irrespective of where they originated – this is an internal market for ideas, innovations and people. An organisation may take a while to achieve such a major culture change.

Creating a buzz

Finally, as well as developing formal processes and events for idea generation, think carefully about how you can create a 'buzz' across the organisation. Ideally people will be excited about the prospect of creative change where key opinion leaders show active and visible support for your innovation initiative.

4 PIPELINE OF IDEAS
Scanning and external sources

Scanning

The process of looking for and identifying new ideas from outside the organisation is sometimes referred to as scanning. It implies the adoption of a systematic approach to the analysis and evaluation of the external and competitive environments. Typically, different members of the team are allocated various roles for pulling information together and feeding it into regular forums for review.

Ask a member of your team for a quarterly report that identifies trends in each of the following areas: political changes such as a change of government policy; economic movements such as inflation or exchange rates; technology advancements causing a discontinuity (step change in performance) in the industry; environmental trends such as health or green issues; legal and regulatory announcements including EU laws and quality standards; increasing customer expectations and competitor performance – what they are doing and why; and opportunities in the supply chain for integration or efficiency.

QUICK TIP **THINGS TO KNOW**
Make a list of the things you would like to know but think it is impossible to find out.

Whilst this information is sometimes difficult to come by, much will be available simply by asking for it. Consider using internal brainstorming sessions with internal experts, searching preferred sites on the web, reading monthly industry journals or attending networking meetings. Once you have started this process, you will quickly identify useful sources of information. (See also T3 in Part D: Director's Toolkit.)

Open innovation

In recent years the term 'open innovation' has been adopted by some organisations to reflect the generation of ideas stimulated by thoughts, ideas, events and facts occurring outside the organisation. This concept has developed quickly as so much information is now available over the internet, and it is becoming increasingly difficult to protect internal sources of knowledge from the competition for long periods. Industries such as those needing significant investment in high technologies tend to use this approach more than others. The objective is to search for ideas initiated outside the business but that could be implemented internally.

There is also a trend to seek to solve customer problems by working in partnership with other complementary organisations. Perhaps these might be businesses in other parts of the supply chain or leading academic institutions. To identify such opportunities you will need to identify:

→ your unique capabilities – what would you bring to the party?

→ the critical needs of your target customers – what is hurting them the most?

→ the gaps in your capabilities and who might partner with you to solve them.

The term R&D (research and development) is also being replaced by S&D (search and development) in some organisations – meaning that scanning and copying ideas is often a better, faster and cheaper way to innovate, so long as it is within the law, of course.

Where organisations choose to work together to explore and exploit new ideas, it is important that they establish an operating framework that allows them to participate freely. Such a framework should cover the following areas.

1 Specific areas to focus on, such as the choice of product and service segments, or market and customer groups.

2 Attitudes to risk and the management of exposure and investment.

3 Protection for intellectual property and the management of trademarks.

4 The contribution that each party will make.

5 The basis on which revenues and rewards will be shared.

5 PROCESS Idea pipeline evaluation

Having generated a number of innovative new ideas, you need to screen and prioritise them, not forgetting to kill off inappropriate ideas quickly but sympathetically. You will determine the number and type of ideas to take further by relating them to the 'performance gap': how vital is it to do something new compared with available resources. Many organisations find that an effective screening process (see figure overleaf) prevents 'innovation overload' where the sheer volume of innovations and ideas from multiple sources almost paralyses a company.

The generic V-SAFE model[2] provides a simple and easy to use way to screen and select new ideas. If new ideas and innovations are to make a difference, they must satisfy five basic criteria captured in the V-SAFE screening process.

→ **Value – will adoption of the idea deliver tangible benefits to the organisation?** This question helps eliminate those ideas and innovations that are good in principle but add little or no value to the bottom line, now or in the future. 'Tangible' means

---

[2] V-SAFE – Innovation screening process, SofTools © 2007 (**www.SofTools.net**).

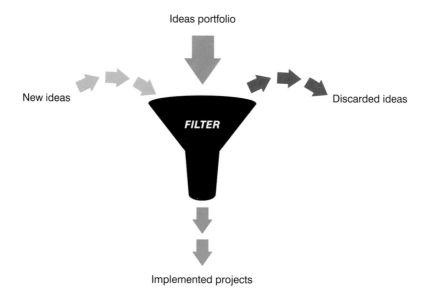

that proponents of the idea or innovation will have to estimate or calculate the specific benefits that will arise as measured by impact on key performance indicators (KPIs), increased revenues or reduced requirements for capital equipment and/or reduced operating costs. However, remember that this should not be too scientific or rigorous as quantification can be difficult in the early stages and can deter people.

→ **Suitable – is it consistent with future strategy and the business situation or context?** This helps eliminate those ideas that are potential distractions and move the business needlessly away from its core business focus. If an idea or innovation is not 'suitable' it still may have value, but only if implemented in other ways – such as outsourcing it under licence to third parties or even spinning it off as a separate product within a separate business entity.

→ **Acceptable – will all stakeholders support it, and if not at the moment, could their commitment be secured?** Often innovations fail in large companies because of the 'not invented here' syndrome. It is crucial that proponents of an idea or innovation spend time and effort on selling the idea internally and gauging the level of support for it. This is often overlooked and failures are attributed to 'office politics'.

→ **Feasible – are there sufficient resources and time?** Can the innovation be managed within existing budgets or will additional funding be required? Do you need to acquire new skills to implement this idea effectively? The answers to these questions will affect the timeline for implementation and the potential return on investment calculation. See it as a reality check.

→ **Enduring – will the idea deliver value in both the long and the short term?** If a new idea or innovation is to be truly strategic it should survive the rigours of time. Is the long-term gain worth the short-term pain of bringing a new idea to fruition? Again this highlights the return on the investment to be made.

The figure below shows the V-SAFE criteria in use within a manufacturer of food ingredient products. The top table simply acts as a reminder to the team of what V-SAFE criteria mean and stand for. The second table shows how six projects have been quickly evaluated using the criteria.

Stage	Activity
VALUE	What is the **value** of this project in terms of contribution to overall business goals?
SUITABLE	Is this project **suitable** given the current situation and strategy?
ACCEPTABLE	Is this project **acceptable** to all key project stakeholders?
FEASIBLE	Is this project **feasible** given time and resource constraints?
ENDURING	Will the value **endure** beyond project completion?

	Title	V	S	A	F	E	Score	Action	Comment
1	Idea A	10	10	8	8	9	90%	Go	*Significantly increases market share*
2	Idea B	8	9	9	4	8	76%	Modify	*Good project but must reduce cost*
3	...	8	10	7	8	4	74%	No Go	*Has only a short-term impact*
4	...	5	10	10	10	7	84%	Go	*Creates significant brand awareness*
5	...	8	9	2	9	7	70%	No Go	*Not acceptable to key stakeholder*
6	...	4	4	3	10	3	48%	No Go	*Non-starter*

Ideas 1 and 4 meet all the criteria well and have been approved. Ideas 3 and 5 have major hurdles that the team feel cannot be overcome (status Red) and so have been rejected. Interestingly, these may stay on the list in the belief that changes in market conditions may make these projects viable in the future (for example, the exploration for oil in certain parts of the North Sea is only viable once the price of a barrel of oil reaches a certain level). Idea 2 looks good but has one major area of risk, and it needs to be resubmitted at the next review meeting once ways to reduce costs have been investigated. And idea 6 simply performs badly and has been rejected. This V-SAFE process therefore not only provides a very fast and effective way of screening ideas, but also provides a very clear communication process so that contributors understand what has happened to an idea and why.

But what about gut feel?

Intuition or 'gut feel' should not be ignored, as it reflects the experience of managers and subject matter experts. If the filter rejects an idea but the team feel uncomfortable about it, take time to explore possible reasons for this. Does the idea need to be developed further, is more analysis required or does the scoring system need refining?

6 PROCESS
Project and portfolio management[3]

Without an effective process for converting selected ideas into action, a lot of the potential value identified during the idea prioritisation phase will not be realised. The process should be simple and easy to follow, but it should also reflect best practice – this can be a difficult balance as one often works against the other. Often the best approach is to identify the tasks and activities that may be necessary for success, but to allow innovation leaders to choose what is relevant for each implementation project. This acts as a checklist. The level of detailed planning required will typically go up if the project is business critical, big (high investment

---

[3] More advanced tools and techniques are available on the Fast Track companion website: www.Fast-Track-Me.com

or a large number of people), complex, multi-functional or spans multiple organisations, or simply completely new.

> **QUICK TIP SUPPLY CHAIN MAPPING**
> Map out the supply chain for your business or team and ask what you would change if you were starting from scratch – what would the 'ideal' look like?

Break down large projects, ones designed to deliver a significant improvement in performance, into stages. This creates a common process for implementing innovation projects:[4]

→ **Initiation.** This stage involves getting the project up and running, meeting stakeholders, choosing the team, allocating budget and resources and agreeing objectives and constraints. This phase will include an outline plan and initial assessment of risk.

→ **Business case.** This involves analysing specific opportunities and threats, identifying overall timings, agreeing the outline solution and calculating the return on innovation investment (ROII). This may be fuzzy early on, but early indicators should confirm the potential return.

→ **Development.** This involves creating a detailed plan, conducting a risk assessment, detailing the specification design and development of the solution, and obtaining the necessary resources and supplier involvement.

→ **Validation.** This stage involves creating a prototype, conducting an internal pilot, gaining feedback from customers, modifying the solution and creating a launch plan.

→ **Scale (go to market) or exit.** This involves rolling out the solution, assessing performance impact, capturing lessons learned, transferring activities to business-as-usual and closing the project.

[5] See the innovation project checklist in Part D: Director's Toolkit.

At the end of each of these stages it may make sense to conduct a formal review where a Go/No Go (kill)/Modify decision is made (see figure). 'Go' will allow the innovation team to continue to the next stage, while 'No Go' will stop any further investment or activity. 'Modify' probably means that the project is sound but that changes should be made or risks mitigated before progressing to the next stage. The structure and rigour required for complex projects can often be helped through the use of managers from other projects to provide challenge and advice – this is known as 'peer assistance'.

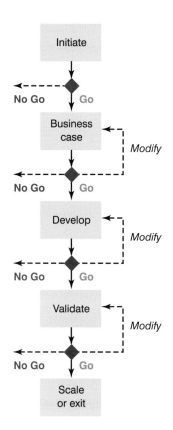

Innovation programme and portfolio management

Whilst the performance of each project should be optimised individually, you will need to review programmes (groups of ideas) and the overall portfolio as a whole. Without effective portfolio management you risk driving one project forward at the cost of a potentially more important project. As an innovation champion you may well have various key roles to play.

→ Ensure that the overall portfolio will deliver against the innovation strategy – gaps and overlaps should be minimised.

→ Confirm that project priority is correct and communicated so that resources can be allocated to the right projects in the right order.

→ Identify, monitor and manage the interfaces between the projects so that critical dependencies are understood and addressed by the relevant project managers.

→ Support the consistent adoption of a common approach to ideas evaluation and project implementation. (If there is no common language or approach then teams find it more difficult to communicate.)

→ Move resources between projects to ensure priorities are met and a silo mentality does not develop.

→ Provide regular reports that show all projects in the portfolio – what are they, are they on track and, if not, what is being done to address issues and risks?

7 PLATFORM *Support systems*

Think about how technology can help with the overall management of your innovation framework. IT systems are not the starting point for implementing an innovation framework, but they are critical enablers. Without an effective system you cannot manage the ideas pipeline and people will quickly lose confidence in the process.

Just like you do for all other core processes, adopt a common approach to innovation through some sort of platform or application. Make a web-based tool available anywhere, anytime and make it quick and easy to use. There are two distinct types of innovation tool:[5] an

---

[5] Examples of web-based tools and dashboards are available on the Fast Track companion website: **www.Fast-Track-Me.com**

electronic suggestion scheme (ideas tracker); and an innovation tracker (based on project and portfolio management) for the overall innovation process – from 'ideas to implementation'. An innovation tracker will present a list of all the existing initiatives, showing how each contributes to current business imperatives, which are on track and if not on track then what the issues are and who is dealing with them.

> → **Electronic suggestion schemes are appealing, as they appear to embrace the whole organisation quickly, but they are also fraught with potential pitfalls and will more often than not die a quick death.** The challenge is to keep the quantity of ideas to a manageable number so that they can be reviewed and acted upon quickly – without this people will again lose interest.

> → **Innovation trackers, on the other hand, tend to take longer to develop and install, but will be more integrated into the overall innovation process.** They will support the implementation process and will result in a much higher success rate.

As an innovation champion, consider your best approach carefully, as you will typically only get one chance to get this right. Fast Track managers tend to start with focused innovation workshops in order to reduce the initial number of ideas and ensure alignment with current imperatives, and will only introduce suggestion schemes once a higher level of innovation maturity has been achieved.

Whatever system is deployed, it should:

> → be web-based and link to a database in order to ensure high-speed, anywhere, anytime access (see figure opposite);

> → provide a high level of visibility over the current and historic portfolio of ideas in order to maximise cross-team learning and avoid reinventing the wheel;

> → support a simple innovation process that covers initial capture, screening and prioritisation of ideas through to implementation and review;

> → be quick and easy to implement, use and upgrade;

> → provide protection for the idea and the associated intellectual property.

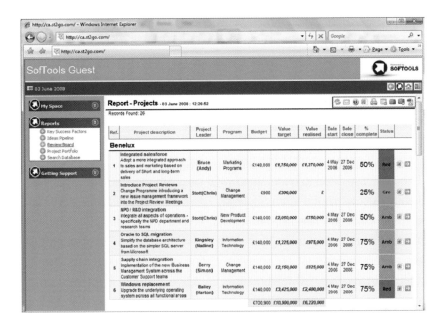

8 PEOPLE Innovation champions

To assist with the deployment of your chosen approach to innovation, think about creating innovation champions across the business. This will ideally start at the top, where at least one member of the executive team will take personal responsibility for driving innovation. At best this will be the chief executive, but at the very least this person needs to be a strategic thinker, have influence over budgets and be prepared to challenge current thinking in all areas of the business.

But it must go further than the board. Each team, whether regional, functional or project-based, should have an innovation champion. This person may be full-time or part-time, but they need to allocate some of their time, effort and energy to the creation of an innovation culture. They need to be skilled in creativity, facilitation and project management techniques, and they need to be recognised for the vital contribution they make to the business. The worst thing you can do is to ask someone to do this important task on top of their day job without removing any of their current workload and without any formal recognition. Everyone should see this role as a career development opportunity, an opportunity to develop skills of significant future value to the business. Pick your best people.

As well as innovation champions, there will be other stakeholders involved in the overall innovation process. Some will be full-time on the task and many part-time. Some will be obvious players, such as the research and development director, and some will be more subtle. We've seen a sales manager step into a project at the last minute and blow it out of the water because she felt that her salespeople could not sell the planned concept. Without knowing comprehensively who will play a role in innovation, it is not possible to plan what can be achieved.

You will also need to understand what skills are required and what skills already exist within the team. To begin with it's almost certain that innovation champions will need some training, probably from outside trainers. A member of the innovation team at a software company, for example, was asked to conduct an analysis of competitors in order to identify potential innovative new features that could be included in the next product release. Whilst he was full of enthusiasm for the task, the starting point was to ensure that he had a good understanding of what competitor analysis entailed.

It will also be useful to identify external contributors that you will be able to call upon – possibly subject matter experts, professional bodies, strategic partners and research organisations. Make a list of potential helpers and choose the best contributor for the task, rather than go to the first organisation that you think of.

QUICK TIP **PRODUCT INNOVATION**
In product innovation, constantly challenge the status quo – be it faster, thinner, lighter, cheapest, etc.

Virtual teams

Most organisations do not have a full-time innovation team. Those involved in the process will work for different functions and may be located in different geographic locations. Perhaps some will be advisers working in specialist consultancies or academic institutions. Wherever they are located, it is important that they are good networkers and can work effectively as a 'virtual team'.

9 PEOPLE *Creative culture*

Culture can be defined simply as 'the way we work'. It embodies the shared behaviours, beliefs and attitudes of any team. In the area of innovation, it will reflect the extent to which the processes and techniques defined by the senior team are adopted across the organisation.

The greatest influence on an organisation's culture is the most senior executive, and as such you need to ensure that they are actively and visibly committed to your cause. Ask a senior manager to kick off your focused innovation workshops and ensure they identify and recognise the best idea in each month or quarter with some sort of reward and publicity. Simple visible statements like this will have a dramatic impact across the business in terms of people's recognition of the importance of innovation. The way the managers and experts respond to new ideas will either encourage or dissuade people from engaging in the process. You need to allow people to make mistakes, and whilst you will always want to understand what went wrong if the project has to be abandoned, you need to avoid creating a blame culture at all costs.

A leading car manufacturer introduced a plan-do-check-act (PDCA) process for continuous innovation and improvement across the organisation. People quickly learned to **plan** what they were going to do or change, **do** it, **check** on the effect it had on performance and then **act** to correct any issues that may have arisen. Unfortunately, after the first six months various people around the organisation had renamed this the PDCAWF process, and new ideas for improvement quickly dried up. When asked what this stood for they replied: plan-do-check-act-witch-hunt-fire! It appears that the management team had not created a blame-free culture.

Consider all aspects of the reward and recognition scheme and think creatively. In one organisation, the general manager was happy to pay £150 for each new idea that resulted in a significant performance improvement. This proved very popular initially, but ideas slowed up as people lost interest. The scheme was then changed by a creative innovation manager so that the person with the new idea would still receive £150 in value, but they now had to spend the money on developing themselves in a non-work related way. Some would do a parachute jump, others would learn a musical instrument, and perhaps others would learn to dance or speak a foreign language. The cost to the business was the same, but the conversations in the canteen were animated and enthusiastic, and ideas once again started to flow.

Think also about how to communicate internally a clear and consistent message. This must go beyond marketing slogans or statements in the annual report. Perhaps you could hold customer focus groups on-site, circulate market reports to a broader community, change weekly meetings to include innovation as an agenda item, or change project review meetings to get the team to look for 'breakthroughs' – ways in which they could dramatically improve the performance of what they are doing. The key is to build consistent messages into the day-to-day activities of everyone in the business.

10 PERFORMANCE MANAGEMENT

Like any other core discipline, you must create a governance structure that monitors the effectiveness of your innovation process or framework. Focus monthly and weekly meetings on the performance of both new ideas and projects. Put in place a process that escalates issues and associated risks where appropriate. Make sure the performance of the innovation process and the issues raised drive and inform the next planning process and review of strategy.

As with other areas of the business, it is useful to develop a specific set of key performance indicators that reflect what you want the innovation process to do for you. These indicators should reflect input (the number and quality of ideas), process (the effectiveness and efficiency of implementation) and output (return on innovation investment) measures, and will typically include the following.

→ **The impact on bottom-line performance.** All innovations need to be evaluated in terms of the contribution they make to the financial performance of the business, or in terms of impact on current goals. This may not be easy, as benefits can be hard to quantify and may continue over a number of years. Think about the appropriate time period for evaluation — most ideas probably need to show a clear return within three years or else you may consider them too risky.

→ **The number and mix of ideas**. How many ideas are you looking for? Suggestion schemes often fail because they identify too many in too short a time period. Often these ideas do not fit with strategy, and there are simply too many to be implemented, so the whole scheme dies a quick death.

→ **The fit with strategy**. Check that ideas still focus on current business imperatives or on future product-market priorities. All too often energy, time and budget is wasted on ideas that distract the business from its current or future core business.

→ **The extent of innovation**. You may have the right number and type of ideas but are they stretching enough? If not, your innovation process may appear more like a continuous improvement process and may not ultimately give you the step change in performance you are looking for. Alternatively, if your current business goals are not very ambitious then incremental innovations may be more appropriate.

→ **The effectiveness and efficiency of the process**. How many people and resources does it take to get an idea through to successful implementation? Some organisations refer to the idea of a return on innovation investment (ROII), which compares the bottom-line performance impact with the investment in capital expenditure (CapEx) and operational expenditure (OpEx) to make it happen.

→ **A culture of learning**. Check whether the same ideas are coming up year after year (which highlights problems with communication processes in that people should know that an idea has been proposed previously). Check also to see whether the same mistakes are still being made (in which case your process for capturing lessons learned and making process improvements may have broken down – see figure overleaf).

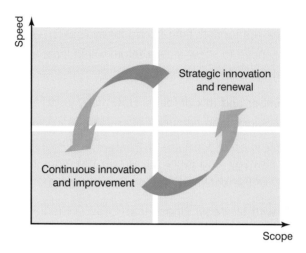

→ **The overall success rate**. A 100 per cent success rate for projects will probably reflect that you are not taking enough chances or being innovative enough. Expect some failures and be prepared to deal with them. However, a success rate of less than 50 per cent probably highlights a deficiency in your current processes.

Having reviewed each individual innovation project it is time to look at the whole portfolio. Does the overall portfolio still link to strategy and are there measures in place to monitor progress? Recognise also that the frequency of measuring performance depends upon how critical the innovations are to the overall business performance. Make sure that the level and detail of performance monitoring across the portfolio is higher for strategic projects than for continuous improvement projects – although both are critical to the overall success of the innovation process.

Don't forget to embed performance measurement throughout your innovation processes and systems. It will give managers real-time information on how innovations are progressing and their performance against the selected measures – which are on track (Red-Amber-Green), what are the issues and who is dealing with them?

The way you conduct your review meetings allows you to create a culture of learning and continuous improvement. When reviewing a Red status project you obviously want to get it back on track as quickly as possible, but once you have achieved this, take time to reflect on what you would do differently next time – could the problem have been avoided in the first place and, if so, how? Make sure that your thoughts feed back into your planning and decision-making processes.

Information technology

Performance management is an area where the use of appropriate technologies can have a big impact and make your life simpler. Create a web-based dashboard that presents the key information about:

→ the pipeline of new ideas (quality and quantity);

→ the portfolio of change or innovation projects (status Red-Amber-Green);

→ the current health of your overall innovation framework.

STOP – THINK – ACT

After reading this chapter you will have learned about a variety of tools and techniques used by the world's most successful companies to optimise their performance in the area of innovation. Some will be more relevant than others to you, and some may need to be adapted to suit your specific situation. Take time now to reflect on the top ten innovation tools and techniques, and identify elements that you will include in your innovation framework.

What should we do?	What tools and techniques are appropriate?
Who do we need to involve?	Who needs to be involved and why?
What resources will we require?	What information, facilities, materials, equipment or budget will be required?
What is the timing?	How long will each activity typically take?

Visit **www.Fast-Track-Me.com** to use the Fast Track online planning tool.

Capturing return on innovation – the learning bit

Professor George Tovstiga

Why do some companies succeed in turning innovation into profit and others fail? Myths and mystique abound. A new vocabulary has emerged to explain the phenomenon. Companies blame the 'innovation black box' for the lack of transparency and accountability. They fail to 'cross the chasm' when it comes to commercialising new ideas. If they do make the crossing, they find themselves in the 'bowling alley' for a moment's respite before being sucked up 'inside the tornado'. The lexicon is as colourful as the business challenge it represents.

In reality, many investments in innovation are wasteful and make no contribution to the bottom line at all. Waste takes on a variety of forms. Wasted time. Wasted effort on overshooting customers' real needs. Missed opportunity. With so much resource spent to so little effect, it's little wonder, then, that innovation is viewed by many companies as an irritating and costly add-on. This attitude rings true across many industry sectors. Companies invest in innovation with low expectations of success. Pessimism becomes a self-fulfilling prophecy when it fails to deliver results. Stoicism and cynicism are the emotional by-products of innovation.

But not all effort invested in innovation goes to waste. Some high-performing companies succeed in generating positive returns on innovation. Moore[6] identifies three such returns, as illustrated in the figure below.

INNOVATION OUTCOMES

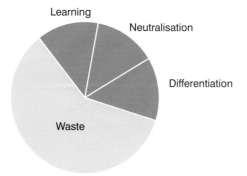

SOURCE: ADAPTED FROM MOORE, 2006

[6] Moore, Geoffrey A. (2006), *Dealing With Darwin*, Chichester: Capstone, p. 6.

Product or service *differentiation* tops the list. In the absence of differentiation, market offerings drift towards *commodisation* and tumbling margins. Few companies find their way out of this spiralling freefall. Differentiation is the antidote. It is how high-performing companies achieve growth, irrespective of the market's maturity. In fact, Moore argues that the very economic argument in favour of innovation rests on the notion of differentiation and its inherent pricing power.

A second-best return is *neutralisation*. This is the best (and only) course to take when the competition has beaten you to the market with a differentiated product offering. However, the sole purpose of neutralisation should be to weaken the impact of the competitor's differentiated offering and to shorten the competition's period of market exclusivity. Many companies fall into the trap of then overspending when they have already lost first-mover advantage – another source of wasted innovation effort.

So far, there is nothing new here. We know that both differentiation and neutralisation contribute economic benefit through enhanced – if not superior – customer value. This, in turn, increases sales, revenues and profits. Undoubtedly, these are two very important innovation outcomes, particularly for short-term positioning in highly dynamic and competitive markets. They are a measure of impact per innovation. Most companies' innovation ambitions grind to a full stop at this point.

For high-performing companies, however, what happens beyond differentiation and neutralisation is what makes the real difference between winning and losing. It's their well-kept secret to sustainable growth in fiercely competitive markets.

High-performing innovative companies have long realised that differentiation and neutralisation are only half of the story. The other half deals with the impact of successful innovation on the organisation – the *organisational learning* outcome. This outcome embraces all sorts of soft, difficult to measure and potentially elusive benefits. Topping the list of important returns from this quarter is probably the development of an *innovation capability*. Innovation has traditionally been viewed in terms of a quantifiable and measurable outcome; the capability perspective on innovation requires managers to break with convention by purposefully and deliberately developing innovation as a strategic capability. Birchall and Tovstiga elaborate on the managerial and organisational implications of viewing innovation not only as an after-the-fact outcome, but also as a future-oriented strategic capability, in their book *Capabilities for Strategic Advantage: Leading Through Technological Innovation*.[7]

---

[7] Birchall, D. and Tovstiga, G. (2005), *Capabilities for Strategic Advantage: Leading Through Technological Innovation*, Basingstoke: Palgrave Macmillan.

EXPERT VOICE

Market differentiation and neutralisation are the traditional ways to measure return on innovation. In business jargon, this translates to 'increasing the buck *earned* per bang'. Organisational learning and capability development, on the other hand, are outcomes of innovation that directly benefit the organisation in the long term. This outcome is a measure of the firm's ability to 'increase the bang per buck *spent*'. Although elusive and difficult to measure, the latter term arguably comprises the most valuable return on innovation and is what really drives long-term competitiveness of market leaders.

TECHNOLOGIES

To remain as effective and efficient as possible, Fast Track managers differentiate themselves by the support mechanisms they put in place to help themselves and their team. These include the intelligent use of appropriate information technologies – enabling, for example, the automation of non-core activities, thereby freeing up time to focus on managing, motivating and leading the innovation team. They may also include the use of coaches and peer-to-peer networks, and gaining access to the latest thinking in their field.

Getting started

Why consider technology?

There are a number of drivers to consider in relation to technology.

The rate of change in the external environment is dramatic. In all industries we see the consolidation of competition, pressures from international markets, emerging new technologies and relentless changes in legislation. How can possibly keep up and remain aware of what is going on?

CASE STORY UNIVERSAL, JOHNNY'S STORY

Narrator Johnny was responsible for the introduction of a global innovation programme within Universal DVD to enable it to compete in an inceasingly technology-led market.

Context Universal is a leading film producer and distributor. It has been at the forefront of the industry for many years, and after being acquired by GE it kept ahead of competitors by introducing processes and best practices in a way that reflected its desire to remain flexible and responsive to the market.

Issue New technologies are impacting all parts of the business, but no more so than in DVD sales, where high-definition (HD) has offered opportunities for growth at the same time that streaming or downloading films off the internet has presented challenges to be overcome.

Solution A key initiative involved the creation of an integrated approach to innovation that included the identification of roles and responsibilities for innovation champions. Johnny immediately focused on recruiting the top people to act as regional innovation champions; after all, if innovation was that important why appoint the B team? He then ensured that they were trained in the right facilitation and creativity techniques, they had a supportive reward and recognition system and they were able to communicate and work together as a cross-functional team.

Learning Getting the right people in the right roles was absolutely critical to success. Appointing second-rate managers, or failing to fund innovation activities effectively, is the surest way of telling everyone that it is not really that important.

There is certainly no shortage of information – frankly, there is too much. How do we sift through the myriad of junk emails, websites, free journals and mobile texts that arrive uninvited at all times of the day and night?

Whilst information overload is a critical issue, the reality is that if we don't make use of relevant and up-to-date information we will fall behind the competition (those that live by the sword will be shot by those that don't).

Whilst technology is not the answer to all our problems, it is a very important enabler to help us remain effective and efficient.

> QUICK TIP **LATEST TECHNOLOGIES**
> Take time once a quarter to review the latest technologies,
> and look at ways to improve the effectiveness of your team.

What activities should we focus on?

Before deciding how to use technology or automation to save time, eliminate entirely low-value or unnecessary activites.

Start by making a map of the current innovation process and then
make a list of all the current innovation activities across each team.
Assess how much time and resource is spent on each item, as well as
the value you associate with each – perhaps using a simple five-point
scale. Then draw a simple two by two matrix to assess where each
activity falls:

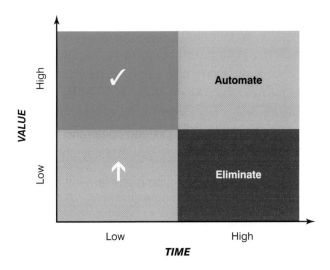

→ Those falling in the bottom right-hand corner are the critical
ones to address – high time but low value. Eliminate these.
For example, perhaps there are idea review meetings you
don't need to attend or some that could be delegated to a
member of your team, which might also be good for their personal development.

→ **Those in the bottom left-hand corner pose a problem.** They are not consuming much time, so are reasonably efficient, but they are not delivering a lot of value. Perhaps there is a way of improving the value of each activity. You might, for example, change the agenda on a weekly innovation pipeline progress meeting to include asking the team to come up with at least one new idea for improvement.

→ **Activities in the top left box are already efficient and of high value.** Perhaps they are already automated; leave them until your next review.

→ **Activities in the top right box are those that make a big difference but take a lot of time to do.** These might include analysis of the competition or market and customer trends, in order to identify breakthrough ideas. These are by definition important and high value, so you do not want to get rid of these activities, but you need to find efficient ways of doing them. 'Automation' may be achieved through technology, such as using a web subscription service to send monthly updates on competitors direct to your desktop rather than you having to search the internet for new data. Alternatively, it might be as simple as changing the way a regular activity is done to reduce time and effort required, such as using video conferencing to conduct monthly idea generation meetings with distributors.

Think carefully about your overall time management: be aware of how you use your time and constantly look to find ways of improving this. Once you have formally conducted a time–value assessment, you will be more conscious of this need. Don't forget that we tend to do those things that we enjoy and put off what is less fun. If you're serious about putting technology to the best possible use, try to overcome this psychological bias and look at the use of your time as objectively as you can. If you do not manage your time well you will find it difficult to fit the innovation task in because it doesn't impact your short-term objectives.

When invited to meetings, constantly ask the question 'Why?' What value will the meeting give you, or what value will you give to it? If there is no obvious answer, then decline the invitation or delegate. The key is to remove unnecessary tasks and activities before looking for opportunities to automate: that way you avoid putting IT and other resources into something that has little or no value.

Finally, encourage your team to carry out the same exercise so that when you are deciding on various options for automation you are aiming to increase the overall effectiveness of the team, not just yourself.

The process-system link

How should we use information technology?

Think carefully about how you will use technology and ensure it links back to what you are seeking to achieve. Perhaps the starting point is to look at your overall innovation framework (see figure below and T2 in the Director's Toolkit) and look for opportunities to make each element quicker, simpler and possibly more fun. Some aspects of the framework will lend themselves to the use of technologies, whereas some of the softer areas such as leadership and culture will offer fewer opportunities.

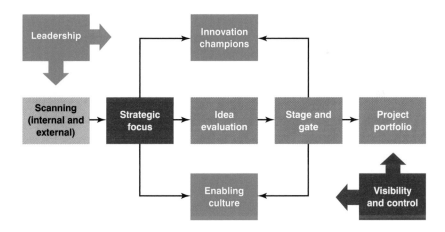

Make sure that the information provided is accurate and timely so that you have the confidence to act on it. Think carefully about security – who will be using the technology, what information will it contain and how sensitive is the data? Most technologies are becoming more secure, but you need to take time to ensure that you set them up correctly in the first place and that you have the appropriate level of security.

Top technologies[1]

How do I know what technology exists?

So now you understand the need for technology, systems and automation and where you are going to deploy it for best effect, how do you find out what is available?

Get into the habit of scanning for technology trends on the web, in industry journals or at trade fairs and exhibitions. Look at what other people in your business are reading – particularly those you most admire. Where do they get their information? Take time to understand what other firms are using – perhaps your competitors or suppliers.

However, be aware that there is a lot of information available, and there are new technologies coming along all the time. How do you decide what is relevant and what is useful? Start with a healthy scepticism. Investigate the technology, but ask the 'So what?' question – is this relevant to my team and to me, and how will it impact performance? As an innovation champion, you may want to suggest using new technologies simply to challenge the thinking of others even if it does not impact on your own effectiveness or efficiency.

Finally, choose wisely – use the V-SAFE criteria (value, suitable, acceptable, feasible and enduring) to make a Go/No Go/Wait decision.

What tools will support a sustainable approach to innovation?

Remember that the development of technologies is moving so quickly that the list of what is available to you will never be static. Use the following list as a challenge to what is possible, but accept that is a snapshot of what is happening at a point in time. The key is to get into the habit of

[1]Suggestions and tips on how to get the most out of technology are available at:
www.Fast-Track-Me.com

constantly scanning this field in search of ideas for improving the effectiveness and efficiency of your innovation framework.

1 Scanning for market and customer insight using the internet

What is it?	By now most of us realise that the internet or World Wide Web (www) is a network of interconnected computers where the sharing of information is made possible through use of a common standard called Internet Protocol (IP). This means that we can gain instant access to information about customers, consumers, competitors and our supply chain.
	There are two ways of getting information from the web – often referred to as 'push' and 'pull'. Traditionally we go to a website and pull relevant information off as required. However, increasingly we can request to have information 'pushed' at us using streaming technologies. For example, many people now have the latest stock prices or updates on the weather sent to their desktops on a regular basis. Others will get competitive product information when it is announced.
Pros	It provides a rich source of information on a variety of topics. The information is often free and you can get hold of it very fast. The internet can provide a wealth of information about customers and competitors in a matter of minutes where previously it would have taken weeks. It encourages creativity, as remarked by the journalist Franklin P Adams: 'I find that a great part of the information I have was acquired by looking up something and finding something else on the way.' There is also the added benefit of social networking with other like-minded people or communities.
Cons	Most of the information contains a degree of bias. After all, someone has produced it for their own purposes. It is also typically unstructured, in that a search on a topic will yield lots of results but the information on each site will be laid out in a different style. Some people call it a repository of several trillion words; the trouble is locating the 25 words you really need.
Success factors	Use the web as a rich source of information and get into the habit of reviewing competitor and customer sites regularly. Beware of information overload, and if new information is of critical importance then validate your conclusions using other sources. A neat rule of thumb is the one that journalists use – only publish a 'fact' if you have got at least two reliable sources.

QUICK TIP SEARCH THE INTERNET
Schedule a monthly half an hour to search the internet for potential sources of ideas and information and make a list of the top five websites to monitor on a regular basis.

2 Electronic suggestion scheme (database)

What is it?	A mechanism by which people throughout the organisation can contribute to a list of new ideas for performance improvement. Intranet technology can make a single list available to everyone.
Pros	It is a quick and easy way of capturing ideas in a single place and provides an effective way of communicating to others ideas that one person or team has had. This often stimulates new thinking or the creation of breakthrough concepts that combine several ideas.
Cons	Too many suggestion schemes die a quick death because nothing actually happens to the ideas – typically because of idea overload.
Success factors	Use an easily accessible database (ideally on your company intranet) to allow people to capture innovative ideas they may have had, but make sure you restrict the quantity of ideas and ensure that Go/No Go/Modify decisions are made quickly and communicated back to the originator.

QUICK TIP INNOVATIVE COMPANIES
Make a list of the most innovative companies you know, and ask yourself what it is that really excites you about them and what they do differently.

3 Ideas pipeline (database)

What is it?	The suggestion scheme is often the process for capturing new ideas and is open to contributions from all stakeholders. In contrast, those more directly involved in the innovation process tend to use the ideas pipeline. It is a database, or spreadsheet of ideas, that provides a mechanism for screening and prioritising ideas, and enables Go/No Go decisions to be made on a structured basis. The pipeline will include fields such as the V-SAFE criteria in order to aid the decision process and to communicate the reasoning behind Go/No Go decisions.

Pros

Once the pipeline is made visible to key stakeholders it becomes an effective communication tool. Use of structured fields will dramatically improve the speed and quality of decision making at the regular review meetings (innovation board). Without a structured and visible approach, the wrong ideas are often selected based on personal bias or level of authority. The person organising the database can quickly detect overlap and competing ideas and resolve the issue before people waste any time and money.

Cons

If the list is allowed to become too big and cumbersome, it can be seen as too bureaucratic, so it is vital that key stakeholders buy into the filtering criteria.

Success factors

Create a single database of ideas based around a structured screening and prioritisation process, but make sure that it is used at monthly management meetings to drive decision making and kill off bad ideas quickly but sympathetically.

Example

The web-based ideas pipeline below shows all the new market, process and product ideas generated in focused innovation workshops. Ideas have been assessed against impact and urgency, and a simple voting system using a star rating is used to set priority.

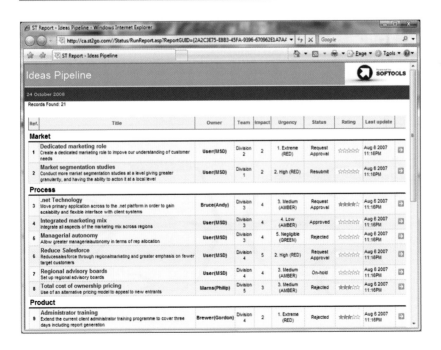

4 Creativity software

What is it?

Software is becoming increasingly flexible and capable of stimulating creative thought – either for individuals working on their own or for groups in a brainstorming session. Products offer graphical or structured ways of generating and developing new ideas beyond the initial concepts. An example would be a 'mind-mapping' software application that would allow you to link ideas in a pictorial format.

Pros

It appeals to people that think in pictures and those that need graphics or drawings of concepts in order to bring them to life. Used effectively, it will increase levels of challenge and creativity

Cons

A lot of people don't like graphical representation of ideas and can find them confusing – in a similar way to how some people love map reading and find them easy and intuitive while others find them confusing and annoying.

Most teams use standard applications such as spreadsheets or databases to view over the intranet to monitor, implement and control new ideas through to implementation. Whilst mapping software can be very creative, the ideas are often not that easily transferred to standard desktop or web applications.

Success factors

Explore alternative software packages that offer mind-mapping and creative idea generation options, but don't commit unless you are sure they are better than good old Post-it notes.

Example

The mindmap below shows the redesign of a company website generated by an internal team. The graphical format enabled them to draw links between the items and to fundamentally change the top level structure.

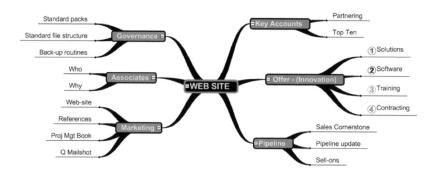

5 Project and portfolio management software

What is it?

Project and portfolio management (PPM) software applications are used to scope, plan, monitor and control the implementation of new ideas using project management techniques. They provide a structured approach to managing a portfolio of complex projects. Most major innovation initiatives can and should be viewed as projects, and they need to be planned as such – too many initiatives fail to deliver against anticipated benefits, often because they are poorly project managed.

Pros

PPM software provides a very effective way of planning the overall portfolio of project activities, making it clear what the individual priorities are, specific objectives and ultimately who does what when. Simple outputs can also provide a clear communication mechanism for all stakeholders. Web-based applications used across an organisation also provide a means for managing the portfolio of projects as a whole, as opposed to managing individual projects in isolation.

Cons

Most project management tools are too complex for innovation projects. They tend to focus on detailed task and resource management, as opposed to the typical success factors such as having clear objectives, an effective stakeholder management process and a simple risk register. It is also difficult to forecast accurately the potential future value associated with a new idea, making it difficult to agree specific targets.

Success factors

Be clear about which ideas can be implemented quickly ('just do it') and which will benefit from project management techniques. Then find a simple and easy to use web-based software product and ensure that key people know how to use it. Finally, don't forget that project and portfolio management is as much about setting the vision and leading the team as plotting the critical path.

Example

The web-based report overleaf shows all innovation projects within the Benelux region. A simple Red-Amber-Green classification is used to identify projects needing attention. During a review meeting, the team will 'drill down' into the detail of projects needing support.

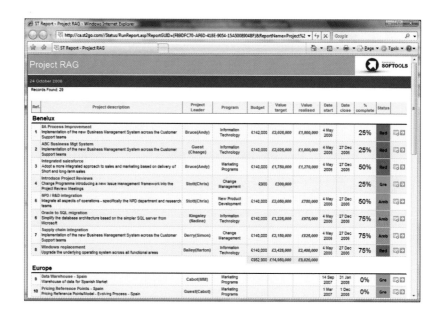

6 Video conferencing

What is it?

Video conferencing allows people to communicate with both voice and video even if the other person is located elsewhere in the world – rather like having a telephone conversation with someone and being able to see them at the same time. This technology has been around for a long time, but with increased internet speeds and improved flat-screen displays, it is getting cheaper and better all the time.

Where this information is transferred over the internet it is referred to as Video over Internet Protocol [VoIP]. Skype and MSN are examples of free-to-use systems that have been adopted by millions worldwide.

Pros

The obvious advantage is that it cuts down on travel, thereby reducing costs and freeing up your time. This will have the greatest impact on companies that have high levels of spending on international flights, but it also has the potential to dramatically reduce domestic travel costs. Some systems will also tell you when the other person is available, and personal desktop-based systems are convenient and very easy to use.

Cons

Setting up video conferencing facilities within a company can be expensive, and many systems just do not offer the quality required for effective communications. They are often very impersonal, and so even when the quality of the signal is good, they do not provide personal contact and can be ineffective in, for example, creativity sessions where resolving conflict and gaining consensus will be important.

Success factors	Investigate internet-based technologies and consider using a standard version in a pilot situation, i.e. within a small team, in order to work out whether this technology is appropriate and, if so, how you want to use it. You will need to establish management routines in terms of what to use and when to make it effective.

QUICK TIP *GLOBAL PERSPECTIVE*

Take a global view on your local activities and recognise that everything we do is impacted by the activities of others, often on the other side of the globe. Use the internet to search for customers, competitors and suppliers irrespective of where they are located.

7 Team email communication

What is it?	Electronic mail allows members of an innovation team to communicate via their computers. This has become the standard form of communication across and within businesses and is a key tool for effective communications
Pros	Most organisations already have email systems, with many being free of charge. Furthermore, even though they are complex, most people have such a high level of familiarity that they are comfortable using them. (When email was first released the CEO of one of the top FTSE 100 companies said that it would never take off.)
Cons	Unfortunately, most email systems are open to a certain amount of abuse, and they suffer from two issues. Firstly, there may be a tendency to copy people in unnecessarily to keep them informed – becoming internal junk mail. This wastes a significant amount of management time and attention. Alternatively, it is easy to communicate one on one without including other key stakeholders in the discussion. In addition, from the point of view of the innovation process, communications between members of the team often contain useful insights and lessons learned, but unless you take action to avoid it, these tend to get lost on completion of the project.
Success factors	Use email selectively to direct members of the team and to communicate with key stakeholders. However, use alternative tools for managing the ideas pipeline and innovation projects, and specifically for capturing the vital lessons learned.

8 Social networking software – blogs, wikis and forums

What is it?	These are special websites that allow people to log in and discuss ideas relating to a specific topic in the form of a discussion thread, where the most recent comments are displayed first. Blogs may be created on the internet or on the company intranet and provide a place where groups of people internal or external to the organisation can share ideas.
Pros	It provides a more open form of discussion than emails, as the discussion is open for others to see and is captured for future reference by other teams. Blogs work particularly well where they are focused on a specific topic – sometimes referred to as special interest groups (SIGs) – and where they are used to solve specific problems.
Cons	Unless there is a clear reason for going to the blog many people just don't bother, so a team leader has to encourage an innovation team to use it and build it into their normal processes. Blogs often work best for IT teams where they already have a culture of sharing insights and expertise but do not work so well with other functions.
Success factors	Consider carefully if you would use a social network, and if so how? How would you focus it on specific business needs or problems? What would make it exciting and worthwhile enough to make it work within the innovation community, when most people will have other commitments to focus on? Perhaps find a small team that would be interested in piloting a blog on a specific topic and see how they get on.

9 Digital dashboard

What is it?	A digital dashboard is a term that refers to the presentation of performance data on a computer screen – whether the manager's PC or via an LCD projector in a meeting. The senior member of the innovation board defines the information displayed on an innovation dashboard. It will contain an update on both the ideas pipeline and the innovation portfolio.
Pros	If set up correctly this provides an instant update on progress every time a member of the team logs in to their PC – 'pushing' relevant data directly to the person with the greatest level of interest or need.
Cons	They can be costly to set up, as the underlying data typically needs to be pulled from other databases and put into a format that makes it presentable. Too often the data is not relevant to the individual user and may not be up to date.

Success factors	Investigate the pros and cons of creating an innovation dashboard for your business – what would it look like, what information would you want to present and how would it support your innovation framework? Once set up, make sure that it reflects the different needs of the different stakeholders that will be using it.

10 Lessons-learned database

What is it?	A central repository of the lessons learned from previous innovation initiatives. It captures basic information about the idea, the initiative leader and the teams involved. It will ideally also present a 'story' of what was done and why, what the outcome was (good or bad) and perhaps what the team would do differently next time.
Pros	It is enormously valuable to the business as a means of capturing insights from individuals and teams whilst they remember and before they move jobs – or worse still leave the business. Without active use of a lessons-learned database, organisations often repeat mistakes in terms of selecting bad ideas or poor implementation.
Cons	Teams often don't invest the time to stop, think and learn, let alone capture the ideas for future reuse by others. Towards the end of the innovation project many members of the team will have moved on to other commitments and they often just don't have the time. Even when insights are captured, people often don't believe that others will bother to look at them, so they are often unstructured and of little value. There is also often a lack of trust in terms of how others will use the information.
Success factors	Make the capturing of insights part of the weekly review meeting with the team, and ensure they are captured and classified in a central, easily accessible database. However, to bring the database to life, make sure that future teams are encouraged to review the database during the initial idea evaluation and project planning phases.

How do I keep balance?

Now stop. Before going out and investing in the latest and greatest, remember that technology is just an enabler. Success will ultimately depend on your ability to lead others, your behaviours and how you interact with others.

Be wary of being drawn into new technologies too quickly – let some-one else make the mistakes, but then learn quickly. Finally, if you do decide to introduce new systems into your team, think carefully about the possible risks – what could go wrong?

STOP – THINK – ACT

You may already have been aware of many of these modern technologies, but you should now understand how each can be used to support the adoption of a common approach to innovation based on the best practices identified in Chapter 3. Use technology selectively to impact on performance in ways that minimise complexity, bureaucracy and cost.

Reflect on each of the technologies presented and ask yourself and the team these questions:

What should we do?	What technologies are available that will help to improve effectiveness and efficiency?
Who do we need to involve?	Who would benefit and why?
What resources will we require?	What level of investment would be required?
What is the timing?	When would be a good time to introduce the new technology – is there a 'window of opportunity'?

Visit **www.Fast-Track-Me.com** to use the Fast Track online planning tool.

Open innovation
Professor Klas Eric Soderquist

Coined by Professor Henry Chesbrough of the University of California at Berkeley, the open innovation (OI) concept provides a new framework for strategising, organising and managing R&D and new product and service development. OI thinking ruptures with the traditional view of managers and policy makers that competitive advantage is attained by funding large, vertically integrated research departments and laboratories, which provide engineering departments with the raw material for new product development while fiercely protecting new discoveries and innovations. The negative side-effects of this traditional approach are numerous. Smaller firms, which often are more flexible, more specialised and more attentive to new technology and market trends, have been disadvantaged as they could not achieve the critical mass of resources to conduct research under these centralised conditions. Cutting-edge technologies were hampered in their development due to patent and protection systems designed for the closed and centralised approach or, even worse, new technologies developed in start-ups might be bought up by the big players and put in quarantine.

The resulting 'band wagon effect' in research and technology development (RTD) is obviously not optimal for stimulating the diversity, experimentation and exploration required in a business environment characterised by ever-increasing technological complexity and discontinuous changes, including a dramatic rise in the number and mobility of knowledge workers and the emergence of RTD-intensive companies in the new booming economies in Asia.

What is open innovation?

Open innovation can be summarised as trying to combine internal and external *resources* as well as *opportunities* for innovation: 'firms commercialize external (as well as internal) ideas by deploying outside (as well as in-house) pathways to the market'.[2] As Chesbrough and other scholars advance, the boundary between a company or a research institution and its R&D stakeholder environment (specialised research performers, suppliers, customers and 'lead users') is porous, enabling innovations to move more easily between the two. More precisely, when guided by OI principles, companies can commercialise ideas outside their internal development and market pathways, as well as using those pathways for bringing externally generated ideas and inventions to the market.

Open Innovation is not a panacea for all industries.[3] Most likely, different industries will be located on a continuum between more closed (e.g. nuclear and military) and more open (e.g. open source software development, mobile and IT services). The more the following five trends are impacting a particular industry, the greater the benefits from an OI approach to R&D in that sector:

1 *Globalisation*, which lowers entry barriers to new markets and gives fast and flexible innovators an advantage.

2 *Technology intensity*, which requires specialised knowledge in deep but narrow fields of expertise, making 'doing it all in-house' impossible even for the largest companies.

[2] Chesbrough, H. W. (2003), 'The era of open innovation', *Sloan Management Review*, 44(3), 35–41.
[3] Gassman, O. (2006), 'Opening up the innovation process: towards an agenda', *R&D Management*, 36 (3), 223–8.

3 *Technology fusion*, which means that traditional scientific boundaries are erased, for example in integrated technologies such as mecatronics, optronics and bioinformatics. The greater the need for cross-disciplinary knowledge input in R&D in a particular field, the more it is important to set up broad R&D alliances.

4 *Alternative business models*, which bring together firms active in various sectors, as required for example in the development and exploitation of multimedia products and services.

5 *Knowledge leveraging*, which reflects the need of organisations for tapping into a broad and volatile base of expertise for their R&D, and for R&D to act as evaluators and brokers of knowledge rather than recruiters and internal developers of competences.

Hence, in industries where the above factors are important, some of them even considered as 'permissions to play', there is an imperative need for developing more open innovation strategies and approaches to R&D.

IMPLEMENTING CHANGE

There is no one right approach to the creation of a sustainable approach to innovation. You will need to decide for yourself what is and is not appropriate for your business and team, and you will then need to think ahead and plan the changes carefully.

Planning the way ahead

At your first planning meeting with your team, look at each of the key building blocks for putting your innovation framework in place. If the gaps are still unclear or you are seeking to make your business 'world class,' then use a structured audit based on the integrated innovation framework.[1]

For most new innovation champions, this first planning meeting will often generate a significant number of areas that you will want to change; but you can't do everything at once, so identify the key areas to focus on. The following example may be wider than you can handle at the moment, but it illustrates what happens when an innovation champion tackles the whole topic of an integrated innovation framework. Depending on your circumstances, you may only be able to handle parts of the implementation.

[1] See Part D: Director's Toolkit.

Imagine that in the initial meeting you have identified the following aspects of your innovation framework that your team feels represent the greatest opportunities for improvement.

→ **Currently the annual business planning process appears somewhat divorced from the focus of innovation.** Whilst there is an overall strategy in place, it does not put into words the current business imperatives that should guide the focused innovation workshops. Specifically, it is unclear what the priorities are in terms of high-growth and high-emphasis product markets, or where the greatest threats may come from. As a result, many of the ideas that are being created in the workshops are interesting but may actually have very little impact on business performance.

→ **Whilst there are 500 people in your part of the business, there appears to be only a handful who get involved in the workshops – mainly from the marketing team.** This limits the number and quality of the ideas coming forward. Perhaps an electronic suggestions scheme that all employees could contribute to might tap into the natural creativity of the people who are not involved at the moment.

→ **Everyone appears to know who the major competitors are but no one really knows much about them.** What is their product-market focus, how do they differentiate themselves, how are they positioning themselves and what are their future strategies likely to be? Without this knowledge you may have no idea of how quickly or how much you need to innovate. Perhaps a quarterly structured analysis of the major competitors and potential substitutes could provide a useful stimulus for the innovation workshops.

→ **Finally, you have noticed that the sales team are selling only a small sub-set of the overall product portfolio – driven largely by the products they are most familiar with.** They say that, because they are on the road, they have no time to access the company's intranet, and so many of the recent innovative products are literally sitting on the shelf. At the same time, you have read that a new technology that links a smart phone to a company's intranet might provide an innovative solution to this problem – perhaps this is worth investigating.

> QUICK TIP **ASK 'WHY?'**
> Get into the habit of asking 'Why?' Why is this product the way it is, why do we go to market in the way we do?

Great ideas for improvement, but how do you start to implement them? Clearly these changes are significant and it would therefore be unwise to 'just do it' (JDI), but at the same time, you need to get on and these ideas might provide an opportunity to make an impression. It is vital that implementing these changes goes well.

You will need to set the team up to maximise their potential to succeed, create an effective implementation plan and avoid the typical pitfalls associated with implementing change.

CASE STORY **COCA-COLA, JOANNA'S STORY**

Narrator Joanna was responsible for introducing best practice new product development and marketing processes into the operations of Coca-Cola GB.

Context Coca-Cola is the world's leading soft drinks manufacturer. Whilst all parts of its supply chain are important, the focus is on protecting the formula (or concentrate) and the core Coke brand. The marketing teams in each region are responsible for positioning and maintaining the Coca-Cola brand as the premier soft drinks supplier.

Issue As market leader, it is often difficult to come up with new ideas for marketing campaigns or creating new products. This runs the risk of allowing competitors to nibble away at market share, often in the most profitable segments. This challenge is made more difficult when competing with good organisations where turnover of staff is low.

Solution To counter this threat, Joanna made a small but significant change to the well-established marketing management process. She asked each of the brand managers to state explicitly how each new product or marketing idea reflected 'breakthrough' thinking. It was now not enough to repeat a campaign that was done the previous year.

Learning   We often think that major improvements in performance require significant effort, budget and organisational change. However, this tiny change in one critical area of an established process affected every programme, and it met with no resistance to change from the numerous marketing experts across the business.

How should we introduce changes?

So, you're on your way to implementing your innovation framework. There's one thing for certain and that is that people will have to accept changes to the way they do their job now. Such change is painful for many, almost impossible for some, but the good news is that some people – who want to take their team, organisation and careers forward – will welcome change for the better.

The first key is to involve all the stakeholders at an early stage. Make a complete list of who they are. Get the senior team together – perhaps taking the time to meet with each individually beforehand. Explain what you are trying to do and what the potential benefits to the organisation are, and get their buy-in. Without that you are certain to fail. Next, deal with the other stakeholders using the reference of the agreement of the senior management team as a spur to their agreeing to push forward. Perhaps you could combine such meetings with talks from subject matter experts, consultants or practitioners in the innovation area.

QUICK TIP REMOVING BARRIERS
Take time to look constantly at your part of the business and ask, 'What are the barriers to being innovative and creative?'

Work out carefully what your objectives are. Ask yourself how you will know that you have succeeded in creating a sustainable approach to innovation and give yourself a realistic but stretching time target to get there. Make sure the boundaries within the objectives are clearly stated so that you avoid the possibility of 'scope creep', an inherent risk in such a fundamental change to the organisation. For example, suppose you're trying to get the company's strategy clearly articulated. Scope creep would mean that you start to do the articulating yourself, risking setting out the definitions of the strategy independently of the senior managers responsible for the strategy. Your objective is to get the people responsible to articulate the strategy.

Once you have the objectives, you're in a position to make a list of the activities involved in achieving them. Take time to identify ownership, timing and resource requirements, asking what is necessary for success. For example, these might be the activities required to implement your innovation framework:

Phase 1 Electronic suggestions scheme

    Activity 1.1 Design a simple template for capturing new ideas quickly and set up an electronic suggestion scheme on the intranet

    Activity 1.2 Make people aware of the new site, and hold a series of competitions to encourage people to get the thing off the ground by submitting ideas, making it clear what the selection process will be

    Activity 1.3 Select the best ones and communicate the results to all key stakeholders – taking time to visibly reward the best ideas

Phase 2 Smart phones

    Activity 2.1 Investigate the feasibility of equipping the sales force with smart phones that allow them access to the company intranet

    Activity 2.2 Conduct a pilot with a few of the team and, if successful, quickly roll out the approach

At the end of each phase of your implementation, stop and formally assess performance – these review points are called 'milestones', where you check that you have achieved what you set out to achieve. Now look at a timeline and produce a Gantt chart showing what is to be done and by when. The example on the next page is based on the activities above.

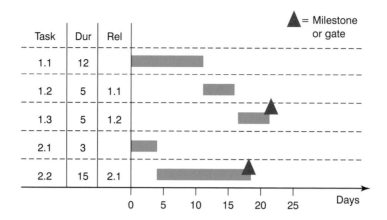

It may be that the other elements of your innovation framework can be implemented with informal meetings with the management team and specialists within market research. Remember, an implementation plan can be very useful, but some activities are straightforward enough not to need one.

So, you now have an outline plan of how to implement a company-wide innovation framework, or division-wide or just for your team: the time has come to get everyone to buy into it by communicating it to all the stakeholders. Avoid surprises wherever possible, so involve key people early in the planning process. You can do this with a conference or a series of emails. You probably need a newsletter, but recognise that it takes time and skill to get it right. Don't do too many newsletters or you'll start to find that there is nothing this month really to report. Eventually you'll find that the flow of information about the framework will be one of the most important roles the innovation champion has.

Produce a report that summarises what needs to be done to set the organisation up optimally. Your report must include some risk analysis, pointing out not only what has gone wrong in the past but also what has worked.

QUICK TIP ADVERTISE YOUR INNOVATIONS

Don't forget to advertise your innovative successes. Your website, for example, should include enough information about innovations to make people curious.

You'll need budget and resources. Work out what ideally you will need: remember that you will have to give a justification for the expense and the resources. It's probably not sufficient to say that without it the organisation will die. You need more specifics and you need to relate it to the achievement of business goals. Look for success stories of companies who have done it before. Point to things that have gone wrong in the past and how much they have cost the company. Look for quick wins – simple things you can do before you get your new budget, or things you can do quickly afterwards. Make the quick wins as concrete in financial terms as you possibly can.

Ensuring success – keeping the plan on track

What approach should we use?

Now you have to keep the project plan on track. Simply putting a plan together does not mean it will happen. Think about the three Ps that you will need to manage: **plan** (tasks and timings), **people** (keeping stakeholders motivated and on track) and **performance** (the project objectives), and keep your attention balanced on all three.

The plan-do-check-act (PDCA) cycle is a continuous improvement approach to managing a project or team (see figure). Use it as a structured approach to monitoring performance and progress and for remaining alert to the unexpected.

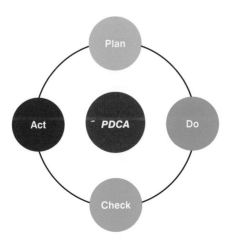

1 **Plan.** You have to plan your activities (you will have done this already if you have a Gantt chart like the one on page 85).

2 **Do.** This implies completing the activities necessary for success.

3 **Check.** You need to check the progress you're making towards implementing the plan. This will reveal any problems in any of the three areas concerned. Here are some examples of what will emerge in the electronic suggestions scheme of phase 1.

→ Plan – a resource that you need will not be available at the time you had planned to have it. Can you change the plan so that the overall timescale is not affected?

→ People – a person you are relying on is getting the tasks done but taking much longer than was expected. Do you change the plan or bring in someone else to speed things up?

→ Performance – the pilot scheme is producing financial benefits but not as much as had been planned. Do you cut costs or search for a way of improving performance?

4 **Act.** Make decisions that will bring the project back on track by resolving the problems.

 QUICK TIP ASK 'SO WHAT?'
Look for the meaning in trends and data from the marketplace, constantly asking, 'So what are the implications for us?'

What routines should we set up?

Complex situations can be dramatically simplified through regular structured review meetings. Depending on what you are looking to achieve, these may be quick and simple five-minute updates in the coffee room, or more in-depth one-day workshops involving all key stakeholders. Reflect on all of your regular meetings:

→ Daily, weekly, monthly (these focus on performance monitoring and issue resolution).

→ Annual cycles (these focus on strategic planning and priority setting).

How do we stay flexible?

Whilst you need to understand the principles of planning and performance monitoring, you also need to keep flexible and responsive to the team, noticing how things are going and changes in the external environment. Think about how tight or loose your controls really need to be. Too loose and you run the risk of missing deadlines and going off at a tangent, but too tight and you run the risk of reducing the team's motivation and losing key stakeholders' commitment.

Nowhere is this tight versus loose leadership style more visible than when a team leader or change project manager uses some of the tools and techniques of project management and gets bogged down by them. Take the example of critical path analysis: this is a useful technique that shows the leader and the team what activities are critical to the completion of the plan on time. You can afford other activities, ones not on the critical path, to slip a bit without compromising the end date of the plan. It's a useful guide for both planning the timing of activities and monitoring progress. But don't get too carried away with it or you risk damping down the creativity of the team and causing motivation problems by an unhealthy concentration on the tasks as you planned them. Critical path analysis can be helpful but in the end it's the people not the tight process that will deliver the results you want. We have known a situation where the project manager was so intent on ticking off the activities on the project network that people were ignoring shortcuts and better ways of doing things just to keep him happy.

QUICK TIP *DAY-TO-DAY ACTIVITIES*
Look for ways to build creative thinking into day-to-day activities.

Balance the team's rational thinking with tapping into their creative talents. Encourage innovation even while you're involved in setting up an innovation environment. You will spot the people who will help more on one side of the rational/creative spectrum and learn to rely on the rational ones to keep the project steady and the creative ones from time to time to take a huge step forward. Some people go from one mountain top to the next one by plodding down the mountain side then plodding up the other one. Others prefer to take a run and a leap and hope they make it. When they do, they have made a great contribution to the team; when they fail, you and the team will have to help them recover. It's the balance of the two that ensures not only success but also the best result possible.

Critical success factors

So how can we increase our chances of success?

As you start to implement your innovation framework, reflect on the factors that will drive success. You can't focus on everything at once, so where do you start?

Whilst your innovation framework may be comprehensive, it should not necessarily be difficult to implement. However, there will be barriers, and success appears to come down to getting the following factors right.

→ Focus on opportunities of high value that fit with current business priorities – this tends to get everyone's attention and commitment.

→ Ensure that the senior team shows *active* commitment to the innovation process. After all, they will have the greatest impact on business culture and if they don't take it seriously then no one else will.

→ Get a balanced team in terms of skills, experience and behaviours, if possible, and ensure sufficient budget and resources are allocated to the overall implementation process.

→ Build innovation techniques into business-as-usual in order to minimise the perceived workload or overhead associated within innovation activity; this is best done through lots of small changes such as modifying a meeting agenda or adding an item to a weekly checklist.

→ Install systems and tools to support the consistent application of best practices across all teams – effectively creating a 'common innovation language'.

→ Develop skills to improve the quality of the work people do in idea generation and project management, as this will improve the overall effectiveness and efficiency of the process.

→ Reward people for sharing ideas and knowledge, in non-financial ways as well as through bonuses.

→ Evaluate progress and performance honestly, openly and with-out politics, making sure that evidence supports your conclusions and that it is presented in a blame-free way.

→ Finally, communicate successes or 'quick wins' to all inter-ested stakeholders so that people can see that the overall approach is working and worthwhile.

STOP – THINK – ACT

After reading this chapter you will be aware that implementing a comprehensive approach to innovation is not necessarily quick or easy. It needs to be planned and implemented using a disciplined approach. Use the team audit in Chapter 2 to identify the gaps in your current approach to innovation. (Note that there is a more comprehensive team audit in Part D: Director's Toolkit.) Then identify the actions you will need to take to make it succeed.

What should we do?	What stages and tasks are appropriate?
Who do we need to involve?	Who needs to be involved and why?
What resources will we require?	What information, facilities, materials, equipment or budget will be required?
What is the timing?	How long will each activity typically take?

Visit **www.Fast-Track-Me.com** to use the Fast Track online planning tool.

Innovation in services
Professor David Birchall

A quick visit to the websites of service providers soon reveals an emphasis on innovation. Nevertheless, innovation in services has traditionally been seen as lagging well behind that in manufacture. Few service providers have big R&D functions to provide a flow of new ideas emerging from developments in scientific and technical knowledge. Few have a well-defined new product or service development process similar to that in research-driven manufacturing sectors. So what is stimulating the interest?

Undoubtedly, not only has competition intensified for many service providers, but also as choice has increased customers have become more sophisticated in their purchasing decisions. No longer can any high street retailer stand still. The utility companies in the UK are subject to competition not only from home-grown companies but also from those acquired by foreign suppliers who have their own best practices to call on to improve efficiency and effectiveness. Logistics companies are faced with fixed-term contracts and rising costs. The mobile phone companies compete strongly on every high street and face low customer loyalty.

So what is there about services that makes them rather different in relation to innovation? In seeking a categorisation of services and manufacture we developed a framework which, unlike others, is not based on organisational features but rather on the degree to which the service is:

→ standardised (e.g. the current account offered to customers by a clearing bank) or bespoke (e.g. the architect-designed house);

→ low in information intensity at the point of delivery (e.g. out-of-the-box software) and high in information intensity (e.g. computer-aided design equipment).

This results in the categorisation shown in the table opposite. This enables the positioning of an operation into a particular segment and then a consideration of strategic possibilities in relation to innovation.

The characteristics of innovation vary across each segment and may take the following forms:

1 **Standardised offering with low information intensity.** This may well be a sophisticated product/service to develop and produce, but at the same time it is simple for the user to develop mastery. Being

	STANDARDISED OFFERINGS	BESPOKE OFFERINGS
High information intensity	Mass-market products/services requiring intense training in operation (e.g. complex software products, complex manufacturing equipment)	Custom-built solutions to complex problems requiring close interaction in areas such as design, operation/ execution and maintenance (e.g. bespoke software, bespoke manufacturing systems, R&D services)
Low information intensity	Ready-to-use, mass-produced goods/services (e.g. basic computer software, games, domestic appliances, car maintenance, over-the-counter medicines)	Personalised services/ products based on low-skilled work (e.g. simple domestic property maintenance, cleaning services)

mass produced for a mass market, to be successful new products/services will have to offer features perceived as novel and desirable by customers or clients. There is likely to be intensive search for ideas and considerable investment in R&D. The new product development/new service development (NPD/NSD) process needs to be geared up to rapid development so as to be early to market. Control over intellectual property will be a key issue in the case of developments based on new technologies. As a defence, where innovations can be quickly imitated, companies will endeavour to get lock-in, and one approach may be 'customer concept innovation' by creating a total customer experience and encouraging repeat business.

2 **Standardised offerings with high information intensity.** Here the purchaser has to be prepared to invest heavily in implementation of the new product or service. The functionality of the product or service will be clearly specified but successful operation is likely to depend not only on the training support of the supplier but also on organisation commitment to continuous development and improvement of operations. There is likely to be a degree of customisation of standard modules but customisation is likely to be minimised to control costs. Innovations from the supplier, which support ongoing efficiency improvement, are likely to be welcome, although radical changes may not be so well received. Incremental innovations are likely to result from close observation of the product or service in use and follow a structured innovation process. This may well involve leading clients in the process for such developments.

EXPERT VOICE

3 **Personalised services/products based on low-skilled activities**. This sector tends to be labour-intensive, and whilst work is subject to waves of mechanisation, limited opportunities exist for technology-led innovation.

4 **Custom-built solutions to complex problems**. These are often one-off projects or distinctive programmes. As such, there is considerable design effort, a tendering process and a complex production process normally involving the integration of systems or sub-units. Innovations introduced at the design stage, which improve project performance without increasing the risks of overrun, are likely to be welcomed. However, if novelty is introduced, it increases the risk of project failure and many notable examples exist of considerable overrun in areas as diverse as building, aerospace, IT systems and defence equipment. A high level of interaction with clients and end-users is necessary, particularly during the design phase, in order to ensure requirements are clearly defined and met. However, suppliers are appointed as 'experts' with current knowledge of innovative solutions.

Many services providers are themselves part of the innovation process in extractive, manufacturing and processing industries. Knowledge-based services such as R&D, engineering and management consultancy have a key role to play in the innovation process, as these organisations have competencies in speciality areas which are likely to far exceed that available to manufacturing or service companies, which only have an intermittent requirement.

One feature, however, of innovation in service industries appears to be a reverse process to that in manufacture. The acquisition of new technology introduced to streamline processes often becomes the source of innovative new services as the potential is recognised. This has been the case particularly with the introduction of e-commerce.

PART C

CAREER
FAST TRACK

Whatever you have decided to do in terms of developing your career as a manager, to be successful you need to take control, plan ahead and focus on the things that will really make a difference.

The first ten weeks of a new role will be critical. Get them right and you will be off to a flying start and will probably succeed. Get them wrong and you will come under pressure and even risk being moved on rather quickly. Plan this initial period to make sure you are not over-whelmed by the inevitable mass of detail that will assail you on arrival. Make sure that other people's priorities do not put you off the course that you have set yourself.

Once you have successfully eased yourself into your new role and gained the trust of your boss and the team, start to make things happen. Firstly, focus on your leadership style and how it needs to change to suit the new role; then focus on the team. Are they the right people and, if so, what will make them work more effectively as an innovation team?

Finally, at the appropriate time, you need to think about your next career move, and whether you are interested in getting to the top by becoming a company director. This is not for everyone, as the commitment, time and associated stress can be offputting, but the sense of responsibility and leadership can be enormously rewarding.

You've concentrated on performance up until now – now it's time to look at your Fast Track career.

THE FIRST TEN WEEKS

The first ten weeks of starting a new role as the leader of an innovation team are probably the most critical – get them wrong and you risk failure, get them right and you will enjoy and thrive in your new role. What do you need to do, where should you focus and what must you avoid at all costs?

To take control, the Fast Track manager will seek to understand key facts, build relationships and develop simple mechanisms for monitoring and control – establishing simple but effective team processes. Again, this task will be simplified using modern technologies and so will become effortless and part of day-to-day behaviour.

Changing roles

Why is this a critical time?

Whenever you start a new role or job, whether within your existing business or joining a new company, you have an opportunity to make a positive impression on others. However, recognise that you will only get one chance to make a first impression[1] – get the first few months wrong and it could impact your relationships with others for a very long time.

[1] Watkins, Michael (2003), *The First 90 days*, Boston MA: Harvard Business School Press.

During a period of transition, the team you will be joining will have few preconceptions. People will typically have an open mind and be willing to try new ideas, giving you the benefit of the doubt. We often see this phenomenon when consultants are called in to resolve a critical business issue. The consultants often say exactly the same things as some of the internal managers, but as outsiders their views are respected and acted upon.

This is typically a period of high emotional energy and activities will often get a higher level of enthusiasm and commitment. Use this time wisely and you will gain significant advantage.

What are the potential pitfalls?

Whilst this period of transition presents opportunities to make a good impression, take care not to get it wrong. Few people recover from a bad start in a new role. You will be faced with a number of challenges to overcome.

→ You will lack knowledge and expertise in your new role and this will make you vulnerable to getting decisions wrong.

→ In every team there will be a mixture of people and politics – getting in with the wrong people or setting up favourites can limit your opportunities for future promotion.

→ There will be a lot to do in a short period of time and you may well feel overwhelmed by it all.

→ Most effective managers rely heavily on their informal networks, but in the early stages of a new job these don't exist.

What is the worst-case scenario?

Because people often give the benefit of the doubt to those who are starting a new job or joining a new team, things often go well for a period of time. If you make mistakes they will forgive you because you're new to the job. This is referred to as the 'honeymoon period'. New football coaches, for example, are allowed to lose the first few games without too much criticism. However, after a period of time (the first ten weeks), you, like the coaches, will need to perform well, meeting the expectations of key stakeholders and winning them over as supporters.

During this initial period, it is vital that you take the steps necessary to set yourself up for longer-term success, or else you run the risk of, as it were, falling into the chasm[2] – you make a good start but then people begin to see what are doing as just another management initiative. Plan your first ten weeks carefully in order to set yourself up for longer-term success. The figure below identifies the need to demonstrate tangible results early on or risk failure shortly after your honeymoon period has ended.

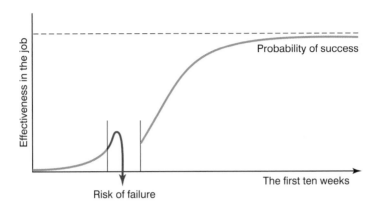

The first ten weeks

What should I do before I start?

Before starting a new project or job within the area of innovation, you need to do your research in terms of what it will entail and what some of the potential problems are likely to be. Develop a personal to-do list of things to get ready or put in place.

QUICK TIP TEN MINUTES OUT
Get into the habit of taking ten minutes out each day simply to browse the internet. Get to know your customers, competitors and emerging new technologies.

[2] Adaptation of concepts presented in Geoffrey A. Moore (1999 revised edition), *Crossing the Chasm*, New York: HarperBusiness.

Think also about how you yourself will need to change. How will you behave differently, what knowledge will you need to gain and what new skills would be useful? Understanding these things will help to build your confidence.

If possible, it would also be useful to identify key influencers in the field of innovation, such as industry experts or your internal director of new product development/R&D or chair of technology board, and start to build your reputation through your involvement in events or discussion forums.

 CASE STORY BOC-LINDE, ANDY'S STORY

Narrator Andy was responsible for introducing best-practice new business development techniques in order to commercialise BOC's portfolio of emerging advanced technologies.

Context British Oxygen Company (BOC) researches, develops and markets products and services based on its in-depth expertise of gas technologies and their application. It is now an integral part of the global Linde Group and continues to be a leading player in this sector of the market.

Issue As the industry became dominated by fewer larger players, the development of new products needed to be more ambitious and on a scale not seen before. This required a more structured and systematic approach that explored different innovation and implementation models – including strategic partnering and acquisition.

Solution Andy oversaw the adoption of the Corven[3] Innovation Cube as the global standard for new business development (NBD) projects across all regions. The model embedded nine key success factors from concept to commercial exploitation. Consistent use of the process was then achieved through the creation of a web-based tool, providing all teams with visibility, control and ultimately confidence over the portfolio of NBD innovations.

Learning Whilst initiatives were of significant scale, Andy made sure that the method of valuing the return on innovation investment was kept relatively straightforward, reflecting the fact that teams were dealing with a lot of uncertainty in the early stages of development and that project managers were not finance experts. Furthermore, providing visibility of the overall portfolio balanced the need to share and communicate ideas with the need for security and protection of intellectual property, a dichotomy effectively resolved through group security settings of the web tool.

---

[3] Corven facilitates the international H-I Network, a corporate and public sector network dedicated to the identification and sharing of best practice (**www.h-i.com**).

What do the first ten weeks look like?

Use the following suggestions to put together a plan for the first ten weeks in your new position. Whilst you will get into the detail of each area in your first ten weeks, recognise that you may be able to make a start before you take the job or start in your new role.

Week 1: Get to know your stakeholders

First impressions will influence the way a relationship develops in the first few months. Start by understanding the key stakeholders in the area of innovation, what their roles are and how each could impact on your success. These will typically include: your boss, work colleagues, your innovation team, functional heads, key opinion leaders, subject matter experts, customers and suppliers.

Do not go into initial meetings or telephone conversations without stopping and thinking them through. What is the impression you want to give and what do you need to do to make sure this will happen? Think about what could go wrong and what you can do to make sure risks are avoided or mitigated. Make sure that initial conversations focus on the other people and not you, so take time to really understand what their agenda is, what their concerns are and what their ideas are for the future. Try not to state your ideas at the initial meeting – it is much better just to listen hard. Indeed it is often said that influence most belongs to the person who says least during the meeting but provides the summary at the end and proposes the action plan.

It is worthwhile assessing each stakeholder group on a power versus support matrix (see figure overleaf). Focus on those stakeholders who have the greatest power or influence over your work and try to understand the politics of the situation. Think hard about how you can win round highly influential people that will oppose your ideas (top left) and consider ways of using the support of your advocates to win round other opinion leaders (top right).

Develop a communication plan that includes face-to-face discussions where possible to improve the support for your team from all the highly influential stakeholders. Finally, do not overlook the fact that a key stakeholder may well be the previous incumbent of the job you are starting. If they are still around and available, take time to learn from previous successes and failures.

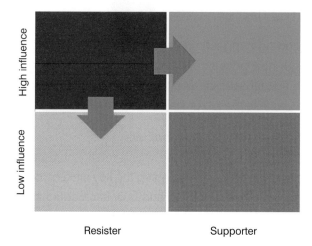

Resister   Supporter

Week 2: Capture a business snapshot

You obviously need to understand the business you are working in, but this should go beyond a superficial knowledge of its products and markets. Get to know what the priorities are and the critical success factors for this current year.

Everyone should understand the basis on which the company competes, but this is particularly critical for innovation, as all new ideas for performance improvement should be linked in some way to the business's unique selling proposition (USP).

Assess the current situation that the business is in. Is it a new or start-up business, a steady-state organisation in a mature market, in the process of rapid growth, a business turnaround trying to regain profitability, or possibly even in a wind-down phase? The current health of the business will guide the focus of your new ideas.

Your quick snapshot should also confirm what budgets and resources you have for innovation and how these have changed from previous years. This will help you to assess the level of importance the business places on innovation. Use the checklist on page 110 to make sure that you have the information you need.

QUICK TIP STOP NON-VALUE-ADDED ACTIVITIES

Look to find ways of stopping individual and team activities that don't add value, in order to free up time to think creatively.

Week 3: Create a team SWOT

Critically evaluate each aspect of your innovation team and identify those areas that you consider to be strengths and weaknesses, and areas that reflect opportunities and threats. Make a quick list, but then prioritise it down to the top five in each category. Perhaps use the team audit checklist in the Director's Toolkit (page 159) to add structure to your analysis, and then summarise your thoughts in the form of a SWOT analysis.

Recognise that this will reflect your first impressions, so some of your conclusions will be valid whilst others may be incorrect. Take time to validate your thoughts with your boss and other key stakeholders – this will provide an opportunity to get to know them better and to start thinking about ways to address weaknesses and exploit strengths. Here's an example:

Strengths	Weaknesses
CEO enthusiasm for innovation Clear innovation priorities for the current year Committed innovation team with sufficient budget and time	No common innovation process across functional teams – inefficient and ineffective Limited visibility of current initiatives Poor learning at end of projects
Opportunities	**Threats**
Cost reduction programme could be driven by the innovation team New product development process needs to be redesigned	Poor financial performance may reduce innovation budget

The innovation champion in this example has identified weaknesses in the way initiatives are managed across the business and the level of visibility the overall programme has at the senior management team level. At the same time, they believe that they have a great team and the full support of the senior manager.

QUICK TIP LOOK FOR EVIDENCE
Analyse the information and the opinions of others in order to get to the facts – seek concrete examples. Making decisions on poor information will lead to poor innovations.

Week 4: Secure quick wins

Accept that you will not be able to fix everything all at once, but by week 4 people will be watching closely to see what you are actually going to do to make a difference. Make a list of your ideas for change as you progress during week 3, and then prioritise them in terms of impact on the business and urgency. Measure impact in terms of how each change will support a specific business imperative, or the difference it will make to overall profitability. Measure urgency in terms of specific deadlines that need to be met or windows of opportunity, such as implementing an innovative change during the summer holiday period.

Then for those changes that you consider to be a priority, identify one or two that you know you can implement quickly, within a few days, and with little risk. These are referred to as 'quick wins' and, so long as they are not viewed as trivial, will do a lot to boost your credibility within the organisation – assuming they succeed.

Think carefully about potential problems and take time to meet with the relevant stakeholders to ensure fast success. You can then communicate these quick wins in a way that builds commitment to the overall innovation programme, and builds your credibility.

For example, an effective quick win might be to conduct a one-day workshop with the different operational teams across the business, and simply capture and share their respective new ideas pipeline. During the workshop ask each team participant to present their approach to screening new ideas, and then facilitate a discussion about the benefits of creating a common approach to idea capture, screening, prioritisation and communication. If successful, you will not only have built credibility amongst a key group of people, but you will also have started the process of creating common practices and increasing visibility of the overall ideas portfolio. Use this as an opportunity to create a learning culture and to show that you are open to good ideas from the team.

Week 5: Create a vision

At the end of your first month in your new role, stop and take stock of where you are. Reflect on what you have learnt and the key messages you have received from your boss and other key stakeholders. You should now have enough information and insights to put together your vision for the team for the next two to three years.

Start at the end by thinking about what you want to have achieved before you move on to your next role, whether it be in six months or three years. The clearer your vision of what success will look like, the more likely it is that you will achieve it. Think about how you want people to remember you after you have moved on: what will they say about you?

Then translate this vision into a team strategy or plan. This should clarify what you will do in terms of the products and services you provide and, perhaps just as importantly, what you're not going to do. Clarifying boundaries helps to focus the team and ensure that your limited innovation resources and budget are not spread too thinly. Then think carefully about who your customers are, whether internal or external to the business, and which are the most important.

Your vision should also clearly articulate your approach to each of the Fast Track top ten innovation elements, as well as what you see as the biggest gaps and how and when each will be closed. At this stage it does not need to be detailed, but it should provide a roadmap stating clearly what you are looking to achieve. You will of course need to take time to validate your plan with members of the team and with your boss. Finish the vision by establishing clear individual and team expectations and performance measures.

As well as putting a plan in place for the team, think about the capabilities you personally need to build in order to lead the team successfully. Where there are gaps, create a personal development plan (PDP) for gaining the necessary skills or experience.

Finally, at this stage you should reflect on the new role and ensure that you are able to balance your work commitments with your preferred lifestyle (and encourage team members to do the same). There is no point in doing a great job if you burn out in the next ten months.

Week 6: Take a break!

By the end of week 5 you will hopefully have done a great job, but you will also be pretty tired. Even the most capable and confident managers tend to use up a lot of nervous energy when getting stuck into a new job. Try to remain calm and avoid getting stressed.

Use this week to take time to relax and get to know the team better. Whilst you will already have got to know your team in week 1, spend more time with each of them on a one-on-one basis and listen to their views, their aspirations and their concerns. Talk to each of your key stakeholders again, and test the various elements of your innovation vision, updating it as you go.

QUICK TIP REVIEW MEETINGS
Get into the habit of asking your team to identify one idea for improvement at the end of your regular team meetings.

Pay particular attention to your boss and get to understand them better. What is their preferred leadership style, what are their major opportunities and threats, and how do they feel your first five weeks have progressed?

During this week make sure you get on top of your day-to-day administration and clear as much of your in-box as possible. Ensure that your email list is under control and take time to delegate non-critical tasks to members of the team as early as possible. Remember that it is much better to deal with issues early, before they become crises.

Week 7: Build your reputation

Recognise that your new role may be fundamentally different from your previous role and that in order to succeed you may need to do things differently. This is particularly important when it is your first role in management, where you will have switched from achieving results through your own efforts and expertise to achieving results through others. Recognise that your personal reputation will now be dependent on the ability of the team to deliver results. Start to look outside your own organisation and identify industry best practices. Seek to understand how you compare with others and with the best of the competition, and what ideas you can and should adopt.

Think about the different events you attend on a weekly basis and how you should behave on each occasion. Check whether you need to attend these or whether there are other meetings that might be more relevant. Think about what you can do to enhance your reputation as an innovation professional. Think about what you will get out of each event, but ask what you can do to contribute. Perhaps there are opportunities for you to take more of a leadership role or to facilitate others.

As an innovation champion your team may well not report to you directly, but may be functional specialists that come together for events such as focused innovation workshops. These 'virtual teams' are often more challenging to lead, so in order to build your reputation you may need to be sensitive to the needs of individual members and adapt how you work with them in order to get the best results.

Take time to build your network. The more senior you become, the more important your network will be to your future success. Your key contacts will initially be internal to the business, but as you become more established, look outside the business at professional bodies. Be critical in terms of how you use your time, as some of the network organisations you can join promise a lot but deliver little, but as an innovation champion in the business seek to identify and bring in novel ideas, new thinking and best practices from other organisations.

Week 8: Conduct your first event

Your quick wins will have given you a feel for what is possible, but more importantly they will have helped to build your reputation as someone who gets things done, and established relationships with key people across the business.

Now is the time to hold your first innovation event, aimed at delivering real value to the business. This is not necessarily going to be easy, particularly if you lack experience of running such events, so personal and event planning and risk assessment will be key. Focus on a current business issue or key success factor and get the right people involved. Plan it thoroughly and think about all the things that could take it off track. Be clear about what you want to achieve and what you will do with the ideas in order to ensure that something will change as a result of the event.

An ideal event would be to conduct a focused innovation workshop, targeted at an issue that people feel passionately about and that is within their power to fix. Gather the necessary information you need before the event to make it a success. You might simply ask participants to think about it beforehand, or you may ask a member of your team to conduct formal research. During the event, ask the team to think about the concept of 'breakthrough', as you want to come up with ideas that will make a fundamental impact on performance – this will establish your credentials for running similar events in the future.

An alternative event could involve working with the sales team to gen-erate a list of the major changes in the customer base. What is the biggest difference that has occurred over the last three to six months and what do they anticipate will happen in the next six months? This will increase your level of visibility and make people realise that innovation is all about improving the competitive performance of the business.

QUICK TIP INNOVATION AUDIT
Get into the habit of reviewing your team against an innovation audit on a regular basis (at least once a year).

Week 9: Reflect and learn

Now stop and review where you are. Take an hour or so at the start of the week to sit back and reflect on what has gone well, what has gone badly, and why. Go back to your original plan or to-do list and then check off the items you have delivered against, and then critically review areas where you failed to meet expectations.

Meet with your boss and ask for an informal review of your progress. Many bosses are not very good at doing performance reviews, but nev-ertheless it is an essential part of continuous improvement. Then meet with your other stakeholders and get their input into what has gone well and what they would like to see changed.

An innovation champion in a drinks company ran an innovation work-shop where 120 new ideas were generated over a two-day period. Everyone who attended the event enjoyed it and considered it a great success. However, just as she had put a lot of time into planning the event, she took the time to seek feedback from everyone who attended, spending 15 minutes over coffee with key people across the business. She learned that the business thought that it was a worthwhile event and that more should be held in the future. She also learned from her boss that the session needed to be more focused as the ideas were not aligned enough to current business imperatives, and that a couple of the functional managers were put out that they had not been invited. She was able to use these insights to plan future events that would generate better-quality ideas with a greater level of support from those functions that she needed for effective implementation.

Week 10: Develop your two-year plan

Over the last nine weeks you have built your reputation and credibility as an innovation champion, you have developed important relationships with influential stakeholders and your confidence has grown. You will by now have an opinion on what you want to achieve based on facts and the advice of experts around the business. Now is the time to develop your two-year plan and seek to influence the strategic direction of the business.

A lot will depend on whether you are starting from scratch or taking over an existing team, but in either case start by reflecting on your earlier vision and update it if necessary. Perhaps you can be more ambitious in implementing an innovation framework, or perhaps you want to focus on getting innovation champions up and running in all functional teams. Then work back and identify what needs to be done and achieved on a month-by-month basis. Keep the plan for year 2 at a high level, but plan the first three months in detail.

Once you have your plan, identify barriers or potential problems that could get in your way. What could go wrong, what could cause this to happen and what can you do to prevent it? Build these actions into the plan.

Finally, you should be as specific as possible about how you will know if you are succeeding. Set key performance indicators that you can monitor on a month-to-month basis that will let you and your boss know if you are on track. Make sure that at least one indicator tracks the financial benefits of your innovation work – what some people refer to as the return on innovation investment (ROII) – as this will help you to justify future investment in you and your team.

QUICK TIP IDEAS DATABASE
Set up a simple database of ideas for your team. Start with a simple spreadsheet or whiteboard, classify each idea as to whether it is a major new insight of continuous improvement and make sure that something happens to each idea.

Checklist: what do I need to know?

During your first ten weeks in a new job, start gathering information that will help you to deliver results, build your team and develop your career. Use this checklist to see if you have the necessary information – using a simple Red-Amber-Green status, where Red reflects major gaps in current knowledge and suggests immediate action is required, and Amber suggests some knowledge is missing and may need to be addressed at some stage in the future. Green means you are happy with your current state.

TOPIC	INFORMATION	RAG
Business context	The major trends inside and outside the industry that will impact what you do, how you do it and your innovation priorities	
Business strategy	The overall strategy for the business in terms of its products and markets and the basis on which it differentiates itself in the market	
Team objectives	The key performance indicators that will be used to assess whether you and your team have been a success	
Stakeholders	Those individuals or groups that you will work with and that will influence success or failure of your innovation activities	
The team	Individual members of your innovation team – their names, their backgrounds and their relative strengths and weaknesses	
Roles	Defined innovation roles and responsibilities needed to deliver results – internal to the team or external contributors	
Customers	Your top five internal or external customers and their specific musts and wants	
Suppliers	Your top ten suppliers – who they are and how they contribute to the success of your team	
Your boss	Your operational manager – who they are, their preferred style and what it is that really makes them tick	
The director	The person leading innovation activities within the business, and possibly the person whose job you aspire to	

TOPIC	INFORMATION	RAG
Key opinion leaders	People across the organisation whose expert knowledge and opinion is respected by others – who they are and what they each have to offer	☐
Current commitments	The current operational innovation activities – what they are and what it will take to succeed	☐
Future workload	Future expectations in terms of what needs to be delivered when and by whom	☐
Budget	The amount of funding available for your innovation activities – where this will come from and what the sign-off process is	☐
Resources	The people, facilities, equipment, materials and information available to you for your innovation activities	☐
Scope	The boundaries that have been set for you and your team – the things you are not allowed to do	☐
Key events	The major events that are happening within the business that will influence what you need to do and when	☐
Potential problems	The risks you face going forward – the things that could go wrong based on the assumptions you have made	☐
SWOT	The relative strengths, weaknesses, opportunities and threats for your innovation team	☐
Review process	The formal review process for your internal team reviews, where KPIs will be reviewed with your boss	☐

QUICK TIP CONSTRUCTIVE CHALLENGE

Get into the habit of challenging members of your team to think differently, to explore options and to build their case for innovative ideas.

STOP – THINK – ACT

After reading this chapter you will be aware of how critical the first ten weeks in a new role can be to success and that there are a number of actions that you should take to increase your chances of success. Take time now to reflect on each of these ideas and put together a plan for your first ten weeks.

What should I do?	What do I need to achieve?
Who do I need to involve?	Who needs to be involved and why?
What resources will I require?	What information, facilities, materials, equipment or budget will be required?
What is the timing?	When will tasks be achieved?
	Week 1
	Week 2
	Week 3
	Week 4
	Week 5
	Week 6
	Week 7
	Week 8
	Week 9
	Week 10

Visit www.Fast-Track-Me.com to use the Fast Track online planning tool.

Global sourcing and innovation

Professor Ben Dankbaar[4]

EXPERT VOICE

Large companies, but increasingly also small companies, have become distributed entities with various activities located in different places. Modern means of communication and logistics have enabled the creation of complex production structures, with parts and components being produced in different countries to be assembled in yet another country and then to be shipped again around the world. Although the geographical distance between these different places can be large, the organisational distance can still be considered very short as long as all activities are part of the same company. Things are different, however, if

[4] Dankbaar, B. (2007), 'Global Sourcing and Innovation: The Consequences of Losing both Organizational and Geographical Proximity', *European Planning Studies*, 15(2), 271–88.

activities are being outsourced to other companies. To a casual observer (and to a dismissed worker in the home country) outsourcing to a factory in Eastern Europe or Malaysia may not appear to be very different from 'off-shoring' the same activity to a company-owned plant in these countries. But for the company, there is a major difference. Outsourcing implies that the company is leaving an activity to another party and will not invest in the related competence any more. Outsourcing therefore is a strategic decision, which cannot easily be reversed.

Surprisingly, there is very little attention in the literature on outsourcing to the problem of long-term loss of competencies. What are the implications of the loss of manufacturing competencies? An obvious place to look for implications is in product development. The type of knowledge flowing from manufacturing to development appears to be twofold. On the one hand, there is knowledge of processing. People in manufacturing know the characteristics of materials and the machinery and equipment used to work with these materials. The second type of knowledge is knowledge about assembly. Communication between manufacturing and development can be seen as a dynamic process in which manufacturing knowledge and new product ideas interact in the development of improved products and processes. Because some of the knowledge is experiential, there is a strong preference for face-to-face communication, but this may not always be strictly necessary. However, if manufacturing is done in another company than development, access to manufacturing knowledge by development people will tend to become more difficult. In the course of time, manufacturing knowledge will disappear from the outsourcing company, while the contract manufacturer is acquiring more and more knowledge that is valuable for product development. As a result, contract manufacturers will be able to take over more and more product development activities and this is indeed happening in practice.

If product development is limited to incremental change and 'more of the same', communication barriers between manufacturing and development may not be so important and development may stay in-house even if manufacturing is outsourced. On the other hand, outsourcing of manufacturing is not an option if a company is planning to remain actively engaged in more than just incremental product development. Decisions to outsource the manufacturing of certain products, parts or modules should be seen as implicit decisions that the company is no longer interested in carrying out development activities for these particular products. Although the development function may disappear later, the decision to discontinue development should be seen as preceding the decision to outsource manufacturing.

LEADING THE TEAM

Leadership is as important to success as gaining expert knowledge and being familiar with appropriate tools and techniques. Focus on your personal attributes as an innovation leader and reflect on what it takes to lead and develop a team.

Changing myself

How should I think?

The starting point is to look closely at yourself and reflect on your self-perception. If you are a newly promoted manager or have just been made an innovation champion make sure you review that self-perception and adjust it where necessary. As you get into more challenging jobs you must move onwards and upwards in your thinking.

All roles are different by nature, but the jump from one grade to the next is probably the most pronounced when you first step into management. How often do we hear people reflecting on how the ace sales representative does not necessarily make the best sales manager? This is the same for any innovation champion. You may have been great at coming up with creative ideas, but can you get others to do the same, and can you lead and motivate a team of people that may not even report to you?

You need to start thinking as an innovation professional. Whilst it is likely to be the most enjoyable job you will ever do, it is not something you do for the fun of it – you've got to make money. We define 'innovation' as the commercial exploitation of ideas, and as a manager in this area you must drive results to the bottom line.

You will also need to be more aware of the whole organisation and be proactive in terms of anticipating change. How much time do you spend thinking about the future? Is it really enough? One of the key attributes of the Fast Track manager is that they will spend more time looking up and around them at what is happening in other functions or businesses.

Think differently, think innovatively.

QUICK TIP YOUR NEXT JOB
Think about your next job and imagine how different it will be, then list the things you can do today to help prepare for this next challenge.

What personal attributes will I need?

The starting point for managing an effective innovation team is to manage yourself. Whenever we see a manager setting career and personal development activities for members of their team we are often impressed by their professionalism. Unfortunately, all too often they have not been so diligent with their own personal development planning.

Conducting a self-assessment against four dimensions is a useful starting point: knowledge, competencies, attitudes and behaviours. Do you have the necessary **knowledge** about changes in the industry, your top ten customers and major competitors? Do you have the **competencies** to think creatively, conduct analyses to understand why things happen (or could happen), review innovation processes and put into place plans that will deliver benefits on time and within budget? Do you have the right **attitude** in terms of being positive, seeking synergies between other people's ideas and constantly looking for breakthroughs? And do your **behaviours** actively support others in the innovation process and do you have the determination to overcome obstacles?

Use a structured approach to identify specific areas in each of the four categories that you need to work on. However, before taking action, take time to discuss your thoughts with your boss or your coach and seek evidence for good or poor performance. Perhaps summarise your thoughts in the form of a SWOT (strengths, weaknesses, opportunities and threats) before putting a plan together. However, do not be overambitious and try to develop yourself too quickly – becoming an effective innovation champion takes time.

QUICK TIP BUSINESS STRATEGY
Make sure you know what the strategy of your business is and focus your innovation activities on the specific imperatives for the next one to three years

What leadership style is appropriate?

These may be your first tentative steps into management or you may be an experienced manager, but in either case take time to reflect on what leadership style may be appropriate for the innovation champion. One way of thinking about this is to consider the extent to which you involve others in events and key decisions. One extreme is to be dictatorial and adopt a 'command' style, where you make the decisions in isolation without involving or consulting others. For example, you may decide what the priority ideas are and simply tell people to get on with implementing them. At the other extreme you allow the group to decide what ideas to choose through a consensus-driven approach. There are of course stages between the two. You may choose to ask questions of key managers in order to confirm facts, such as the threat from the competition, or you may consult them individually or as a group and ask their opinion – but then still make the decisions yourself. This model of innovation leadership is effectively a continuum from command to consensus, as shown in the figure overleaf.

So is there a preferred style for the innovation champion? The reality is that there is no one right or wrong answer and that your choice will vary depending on the situation. Fast Track innovation champions assess each situation quickly and are then flexible enough to adapt their style based on three criteria.

The first is **time**. Involving others (moving from command to consensus on the continuum) increases both the time delay in the decision and

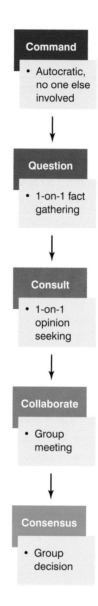

Command
- Autocratic, no one else involved

Question
- 1-on-1 fact gathering

Consult
- 1-on-1 opinion seeking

Collaborate
- Group meeting

Consensus
- Group decision

the number of people and time involved in the decision-making process. This can cause serious delays when choices need to be made quickly. The second is **commitment**. So long as the team respect their manager, the more involved people feel the more likely they are to commit to decisions and actively support the implementation of new ideas. The third dimension is **quality**. There is no point making decisions in isolation if you lack the facts or experience – you will simply be risking the failure of the idea and exposing your reputation. At the same time, if you are to allow the team to make the final Go/No Go decisions and to set priorities, you need to make sure that whatever they come up with will be acceptable to the business. Be clear about the boundaries in terms of timings and outcomes, and limitations in terms of what would and would not be an acceptable solution – they can be as tight or as loose as is appropriate, but once set you will find them very difficult to change. People get used to a manager's style and adapt their behaviour to conform, or move out if they don't like it. Once they have experience of your style they may well be uncomfortable if you try to change it. Of course, you will change your style according to the situation and they will appreciate that and why you are doing it. You can't use a collaborative style when there's a fire in the factory and you're in charge, but it may be appropriate to spend a lot of time with the team discussing how to put things back to normal when the fire is out.

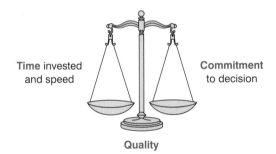

Time invested
and speed

Commitment
to decision

Quality

Reflect on your style of leadership using the simple model below. What is your preferred style? When would a consensus style be more appropriate and when would a command style be more effective? Whilst everyone has a preferred style, Fast Track innovation champions are comfortable operating at all points on the continuum, but to do this they will have developed appropriate skills.

→ **Command.** Ability to analyse the situation, solve problems alone, make decisions, proactively think ahead and manage risks, and the willingness and ability to tell others what to do.

→ **Question.** Ability to ask open and closed questions and, most importantly, listen to the answers without interrupting, to the point where you have sufficient facts to make the decision.

→ **Consult.** Willingness and ability to listen hard to what others are telling you. Ability to listen to subtler signals, such as feelings and opinions, and the ability to seek proposals from others and integrate into decisions.

→ **Collaborate.** Ability to manage meetings effectively with clear objectives, agenda and logistics. Willingness to challenge the group, discuss ways forward and manage conflict where there are differences of opinion

→ **Consensus.** Ability to set group boundaries, facilitate discussion, build consensus in a team and gain commitment to outputs. (Remember that not everyone needs to agree with the decision of the group, but they do need to commit to it.)

Coaching

Whilst not part of the formal leadership model above, coaching should play a role in developing yourself as well as members of your team. It is said that if you want to master a particular discipline then teach it. Fast Track managers develop excellent coaching skills and are in turn prepared to be coached – helping individuals develop core skills or resolve barriers.

 CASE STORY SAUDI TOURISM COMMISSION, MANSOUR'S STORY

Narrator Mansour worked with the Commission to introduce best practice project and programme management techniques into a newly formed and entrepreneurial team.

Context In order to reduce its dependency on oil, the Saudi Arabian government took the decision to create a tourism industry. Over a 15-year period, it intended to focus on both the demand (marketing of tourism destinations and activities) and supply (development of new tourist resources). It would focus initially on domestic and religious tourism and then move on to international tourism.

Issue Due to the scope and scale of the programme there were a significant number of stakeholders interested and involved, both inside and outside the country. This resulted in an overwhelming number of ideas for developing new services and creative ways of marketing them. So the key challenges faced by Mansour and the team were to prioritise ideas heavily (what would have the greatest impact and be feasible to implement) and ensure effective follow-through to practical implementation on the ground.

Solution The Commission decided to adopt a common project management process and web-based system to ensure a consistent yet simple approach to the definition, planning, implementation and control of innovation projects. With Mansour's help, it integrated a planning template (a 'project passport') with an online coach so that inexperienced project managers could get up to speed quickly.

Learning Whilst the approach was considered simplistic by many, for others it represented a giant leap forward. Different stakeholders were able to contribute at the level that was appropriate to them whilst all felt part of one extended team.

Motivating the individual

How do I get the most out of each member of my innovation team?

Whether people across the business report to you or are simply contributors to your innovation activities, think carefully about how you will keep them motivated and how to maximise their contribution to the generation of ideas and the implementation of innovation projects. Firstly, focus on the **behaviour** you are looking for. It may be that you want people to volunteer at least one idea a month, or to participate in the innovation workshops, or simply to feed back information about changes in the market to the relevant department. Whatever it is, people's behaviour will be determined by what comes before they need to do the task, called **antecedents**, and what comes afterwards, **consequences**, as shown in the figure overleaf.

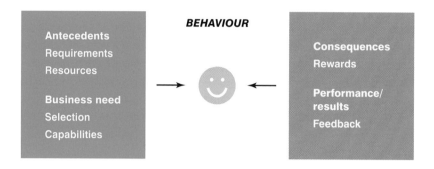

→ **Antecedents.** Once you are sure you have chosen the right people for the task, set them up for success by making it clear what is expected of them and what the outcomes should look like. Targets should be stretching but should not over-stretch individuals, as this can be demotivating. The target should reflect the business need you are looking to address, whether it relates to the development of a new product or finding a creative way to open up a new market. Check that individuals have the necessary skills, knowledge and experience, and arrange personal development activities for those that need it. Finally, think about the resources they will need to be effective. These may include time, facilities, materials, equipment, information and budget.

→ **Consequences.** Look closely at each task and assess the natural consequences for each person. If they do a great job, what happens to them or what benefits do they receive? Avoid situations where there are positive consequences for doing a bad job. For example, if someone fails to implement a new idea effectively because they are keen to move on to a different project, find a way of ensuring this does not happen. Conversely, think of ways to use consequences to drive positive behaviour. For example, if someone arrives late for the start of an innovation workshop, ask them to capture the ideas on the flip chart or to take the notes. The most effective way of keeping people motivated is typically through the use of natural (non-financial) rewards, such as providing opportunities for personal development, allowing people to present to senior managers, seeing an idea through to completion or simply taking the time to stop and say 'thank you'.

Think about the next innovation workshop you will be running and use the model to check that you are set up for success. What do you need to put in place in terms of antecedents, and what do you need to do to ensure that the consequences of participating are positive ones? For example:

Antecedents	→ Ensure the workshop is focused on a current business imperative
	→ Put together an invitation to attend that includes your vision, a set of objectives and an agenda with timing (allow enough time)
	→ Invite the right people to get the right skills and ensure they understand the processes you will be using – hold a five-minute conversation with each to clarify expectations
	→ Ensure roles are clearly defined – such as the administrator and facilitator
	→ Ask a member of your team to gather market and customer insights in order to stimulate and challenge the team
	→ Ensure the room you have is large enough, has plenty of natural light, encourages creativity and has the appropriate layout
	→ Send an email reminder out a few days beforehand asking all participants to clear their diaries
	→ Think about the risks – what could go wrong – and plan mitigating actions
Behaviour	→ The team generates new ideas for performance improvement focused on a current business priority
	→ 'Success' would be one new idea that would make a difference to performance that could be implemented within the following quarter
Consequences	→ Allow the team to present their ideas to the senior manager at the end of the session
	→ Allocate a budget for a team dinner as a way of encouraging future participation and celebrating success
	→ Arrange for someone else to capture the outputs and circulate them to the team within a couple of days

Create the right environment

Why is this important?

You and your team may be developing highly innovative and valuable new ideas for the business, but without a supportive culture key stake-holders will not 'buy in', and your ideas will become just another initiative that quietly disappears. Even though you've given the new ideas the best chance of success by following a professional process and gathering the right data, you still have to take the key indivduals with you or it can all quickly fall apart.

An environment that is suitable for effective innovation depends on the culture you create as the leader of your team and the physical environment that people work in. Both must work together to support the creative generation of ideas and the rigorous implementation of projects – for innovation to flourish and be a success both of these components are necessary.

QUICK TIP INNOVATION NETWORK
Use your network and that of your team, as great innovations and ideas often come from outside the workplace.

What culture is best?

There is no one right answer to this, and it will vary depending on your preferred style and the business context or situation at a point in time. However, there are basic components that tend to result in an environment that will be more conducive to creative thought and the commercial exploitation of ideas.

→ **Creative challenge**. Create an environment of challenge and confrontation, but make sure that it is positive. It is easy to knock an idea, but make sure when you or a member of the team does that you have an alternative or are prepared to search for one. As an example, an experienced innovation champion talks about the three roles that people could fulfil when taking part in an idea generation workshop – called the three Ts. Ideally, she is keen to get people to think about ways in which they could **transform** the business – finding new products, markets or processes. However, the reality is that some people turn up for a day away from their job, possibly off-site with their friends and a nice meal – she calls these the **tourists**. The third T are the people who always have other things to be doing, 1,000 emails to be getting on with and are also intent on finding the day a complete waste of time – she refers to these people as **terrorists**! By making these three roles explicit at the beginning of the workshop, she is able to get most of the team to focus on being transformers.

→ **Blame-free**. When generating ideas there is always a degree of uncertainty and risk. This means that people will not always get it right, and not all ideas will be good ideas. Where ideas are heavily criticised, people quickly stop putting forward new concepts for fear of being ridiculed. Here's a good, and real, example of this: an executive at a US car manufacturer put forward an idea for a new car engine that would potentially steal a march on the competition. However, after nine months and $30 million in capital investment, the engine was pronounced a failure and withdrawn from the innovation portfolio. Two weeks later the executive was called in to see the CEO at a board meeting. Fearing the worst, he apologised to the board and stated that he fully understood if they'd called him in to 'let him go'. To his surprise, the chief executive stated, 'Let you go? We've just spent $30 million educating you – why would we let you go?' The key is obviously to accept that new ideas are about the future, and the future is uncertain – be prepared, indeed encourage people, to take risks and make mistakes.

→ **Search and development**. Historically, only those organisations that could invest a significant amount of funds into research and development would create new products. However, the availability of information over the internet, the freedom with which people move between jobs and companies and the need to dramatically reduce time-to-market has resulted in a new way of working. This is referred to as 'search and development', and makes a clear statement to all those involved in the innovation process that it is OK to reuse the ideas of others. A good illustration of this is Richmond Ice Cream, the UK's largest manufacturer of ice cream. When faced with overwhelming competition from a dominant international brand, Walls, Richmond made a clear choice to focus on its operational effectiveness so that it could replicate or counter any product Walls brought out within a matter of weeks. James Lambert, the Richmond CEO, talks about the vital role of 'strategy, strategy, strategy' – for Richmond at the time it meant doing what someone else was already doing, but doing it faster, better and cheaper. This is a good example of staying ahead in a niche market dominated by a big player.

→ **Ethical**. Make a choice about what you will and will not be prepared to consider. As well as making a statement about your beliefs – what is right, and what is wrong – you will also clarify the boundaries for others. When Nokia moved into downloadable software games for their handsets, the focused innovation workshop looking at new ideas for this emerging market were told very clearly *not* to look at games involving gambling. In any industry there will be the possibility of cutting corners, flirting with legality and, for example, behaving in a more or less green manner. Think about the issues that affect you and your industry and make decisions on the limits you will set. This is particularly relevant when dealing with developing economies.

→ **Learning organisation**. Work hard to create a culture where people learn from each other and from the past. Innovation is about creating new ideas, but there is nothing more demoralising than coming out with a new idea that fails badly in the marketplace, only to find that someone else had already made the very same mistake several years earlier. This is a discipline that needs to be built into the culture of the team. A Japanese mobile phone manufacturer developed a new phone that combined advanced software with the latest thin screen technology to create a display that was second to none. Unfortunately, once released it quickly became clear that the mechanism for embedding the display in the phone was faulty, and almost 50 per cent of the phones had to be recalled. This cost the business approximately $5 million in rejects and $5 million in terms of the adverse impact on the brand. But in the spirit of the blame-free culture, the senior management team stated that this was understandable for a leading technology company – there would be some failures. However, nine months later the upgrade to the phone was released, and whilst it had some highly innovative new features, it still had the same fault as the original phone. At this point the senior management team came together and agreed that an effective means of capturing and sharing 'lessons learned' was needed!

What should the physical environment look like?

Most organisations do not have an innovation function, so a lot of innovation activity takes place in the normal course of events – when a salesperson is meeting a customer, for example, or when people are chatting over the water cooler or having a drink after work. There is a place, however, in probably every organisation to hold structured focused innovation workshops. Whenever a group of people get together to come up with creative ideas and screen them through a series of structured criteria, the physical environment can make a significant difference to the overall outcome. Make sure that focused innovation workshops are held off-site so that day-to-day events such as emails do not distract the group; ask for a large room so people can move around, and make sure there is plenty of light. An innovation champion in a food company tried holding an innovation session for ten people in their operations room – an internal room with grey walls and a notice board, approximately 3m × 3m and with no windows. After 30 minutes there was no air, no enthusiasm and no new ideas. We wonder why?

Once the physical conditions are right, make sure you are ready to capture new ideas as and when they come. Depending on the group, you may choose to use a computer with mind-mapping software connected to a projector screen, or you may choose to use Post-it notes stuck to the wall. In either case, make sure that the process of capturing, consolidating and screening the ideas does not get in the way of creativity.

Make sure the vital rule of team planning is in place – the team leader must not impose their thoughts on the team. It is a fact that the best idea may well come from the most junior member of the team – after all, they are the people least likely to believe that the way we have done things for years must be right. If the team doesn't think they will be listened to unless their view accords with the leader's, they will soon stop contributing.

Building the team

What makes a great team?

So you have a great leadership style that is flexible enough to cope with different situations, and you have a number of highly motivated and skilled people to work with, but that does not necessarily make them a great team. So what do the successful innovation teams do that differentiates them from average performers? Read through the following checklist and reflect on what you need to do as leader of the team in order to ensure success.

→ **The team will have great clarity in its goals and have a real sense of shared purpose.** Fast Track teams will have such clarity of vision that they will know how they want to be remembered long after they have been disbanded. For example, a focused innovation workshop can potentially be remembered as the time when the team developed the new product ideas that transformed the company's fortunes.

→ **The team will have a strong and enthusiastic leader who provides direction, is supportive of team members and is willing to shoulder responsibility when things do not go according to plan.** The leader is often not the expert or specialist, but they understand how to bring experts together and get them to perform effectively as a unit. Members will be empowered to take action and be willing to take on the leadership role themselves as and when required.

→ **Fast Track teams also accept that things will change and can act flexibly in order to bring things back on track.** Perhaps an innovation team is implementing a major change programme and within the first week a key member of the team leaves. They will reappraise the situation quickly but calmly, explore creative options for dealing with the situation and move on.

→ **They will have shared values and a common set of operating principles.** Whilst teams comprise people with a variety of skills and experiences, they need to be unified by common beliefs. We see the enormous power that the adoption of a common set of religious beliefs can have for both positive and negative ends, and whilst levels of fanaticism are rarely positive, shared values will often provide the team with enormous energy and commitment.

→ **Ideally, the shared values then extend into a general respect and liking for each other, where members of the team trust each other and genuinely have fun working together.** The Armed Forces will always ensure that their teams spend time gaining shared experiences in a safe environment before they are asked to put their lives on the line.

→ **There will be issues to deal with, but the Fast Track teams will manage these quickly and sensitively before they become crises.** To do this they need to have open and honest communication and work in a blame-free environment where rewards for success are shared

→ **Whilst these teams will focus on their primary objectives, they will have a feeling of shared responsibility and be supportive of each other.** They will take time out to continuously learn and develop new skills – both individually and as a team. This necessitates keeping an eye on how they are performing and scanning other similar teams in order to identify alternative approaches that could be adopted.

→ **Finally, the team will be balanced in terms of the skills and capabilities of team members and in terms of the roles they each fulfil.** The team will have people capable of creative challenge, but it also needs people willing to get their heads down in order to put the work in and deliver the results. You may want to allocate them roles reflecting different ways of thinking as shown in Edward de Bono's[1] 'six hats' (see figure). You may not wish to allocate these roles, but reflecting on which of your team members operate naturally in one of these hats will help you to make the most of your people and plug potential gaps.

	• White	Focus on evidence and the facts
	• Red	Focus on emotion and gut feel
	• Yellow	Focus on the positive – why it will work
	• Green	Focus on lateral thinking and brainstorming
	• Black	Focus on the negative – devil's advocate
	• Blue	Focus on evaluation – pros and cons

How should I develop the team?

As well as developing the skills of individual members of your team, you need to build them into a strong and effective team. Review the list of attributes of a great team above and make a note of any area where you feel there is a need for improvement.

Next, assess where you think the team is now in terms of their stage of development. This is particularly important for those working in the area of innovation, as teams are often part-time – coming together for events such as innovation workshops or implementation of an initiative. Each team will go through various stages of development, and your role as the leader will be to recognise where they are and to take action to move them to a state where they are their most productive. Consider the following 'forming to mourning' model.[2]

[1] de Bono, Edward (1986), *Six Thinking Hats*, Harmondsworth: Viking.
[2] Concept developed by Bruce Wayne Tuckman in the short article 'Developmental sequence in small groups', 1965 (**www.infed.org/thinkers/tuckman.htm**).

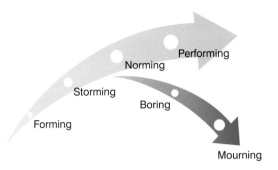

STAGE	DESCRIPTION	LEADERSHIP ACTIONS
Forming	The group is brought together for the first time and needs to spend time understanding each other and what they are each contributing. This is typical of a focused innovation workshop that comprises members from a variety of functions that do not usually work together, but it will also happen with implementation teams.	Think carefully about whom to involve in each team and make sure there is a balance in terms of different roles, skills and experience. Allow people to get to know each other personally and set simple tasks to allow them to work together for the first time and get a quick win.
Storming	Initially they will each be keen to contribute and will want to have their say in terms of who fulfils which role and who will have the greatest sway over the outcomes. If this is not managed carefully, teams can become very 'political', where individuals jockey for power and positions. This can result in a downward spiral in terms of effectiveness.	Make sure that the early tasks the team undertakes are straightforward and will result in success. Establish team roles and communicate them clearly so that everyone knows what their contribution is. There will always be the potential for conflict, so look for it and seek consensus on key decisions at an early stage.
Norming	As things settle down, the team needs to adopt norms in terms of how they work together. This will need to cover decision making, communication and meeting disciplines. Without common processes a lot of the energy and enthusiasm of the team can be dissipated.	Be clear about what will happen at each meeting and that there are agreed objectives, an agenda with timings and appropriate resources. Communicate your leadership style in terms of the circumstances in which you will seek the team's views.
Performing	The team should now have clear roles and be working effectively as a unit. This is where results are produced, and you need to keep the team in this positive and effective mode.	Monitor performance regularly and take swift action to resolve issues before they become crises. Spend one-on-one time with each member of the team to keep them motivated.

STAGE	DESCRIPTION	LEADERSHIP ACTIONS
Boring	For teams that have been together for a long time, there is a danger that they stop challenging the way they work. This is common on major projects where individuals can easily get into a rut. If left unnoticed, it can result in the team getting bored, and performance can quickly fall off.	Find ways of constantly challenging the team as a whole and as individuals. Consider bringing in new members or rotate jobs and roles. Perhaps there will come a point where you need to fundamentally adjust the team's objectives in order to get them to stop and re-evaluate what they are doing.
Mourning	Finally, for high-performing teams there is always a major sense of loss when a valued member moves on. Even if their replacement appears to have the right profile, there can be resistance and the team effectively moves back into the 'forming' stage.	When people leave the team, for good or bad reasons, think carefully about the transition. Focus on some of the softer people issues within the team – not simply on updating the plan.

How do I overcome barriers to change?

Innovation is all about change. New ideas relate to changing products, modifying the way you go to market, altering the supply chain, or even closing down parts of the operation. Recognise that the ideas you and your team generate may be worthwhile, but accept that there will be resistance simply because some people do not like change. The denial, resistance, exploration, commitment (DREC) change model (see figure) can help you

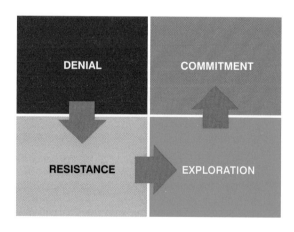

to understand the process that people need to go through and can suggest what you will need to consider when planning changes:

→ **Denial**. People believe that the current situation is perfectly acceptable and refuse to accept that the change is needed or that change will happen. Perhaps the innovation is to shut down the customer services department and outsource it to a specialist company or overseas. You hear the cry of 'It will never happen' coming from different teams. Most organisations regularly fail to implement changes effectively and the organisation reverts back to its former state quite quickly. It is perhaps no wonder that people are often cynical and will wait to see if anything actually happens. As an innovation champion suggesting change, your reputation is on the line. To be taken seriously you have to drive the change through. Accept that some people will be in denial, but find a way of helping them to come to terms with the fact that the change will happen.

→ **Resistance**. Even once people have accepted that the change will happen, many are still resistant. It is their way of telling you that they are still not convinced that this is the right way to go. Work out counter-arguments in advance, take time to explain the business case for the change and make it clear why the current situation will not endure. Identify those people in the business who have bought in to the idea and who are also widely respected – we call them the key opinion leaders. Use these people to spread the word and explain to others why this change, whether it be the development of a new product or the expansion into a new market, is so vital for the future. Experience has shown that if 20 per cent of key opinion leaders are positive about the change, you will probably be able to drive it through; with less than that you may have problems to overcome.

→ **Exploration**. Once there is an acceptance that the change will happen and that it is a good thing, allow people to investigate ways in which it will impact them and their teams for the better, and ways in which they can help with implementation. Get them involved, allow them to ask questions and make sure they are taking action.

→ **Commitment**. Finally, as people start to realise the benefits take time to capture the early victories, write them up and communicate them across other teams. Often, those that showed the greatest level of resistance, once converted, become your best advocates.

The DREC cycle is a useful way of understanding the natural stages we all go through when faced with change. Some of us will move through the cycle much faster than others, so take time early on to help those who are struggling to move through the cycle.

QUICK TIP COMMUNICATING BENEFITS
Don't bore people with minute details and lists of small features, but focus on what is important and the unique selling proposition of the idea.

STOP – THINK – ACT
This chapter has presented ideas for managing and developing your team. This will be key to your success as you will not be able to achieve your objectives working alone, and in the area of innovation, idea generation and project implementation is often achieved via cross-functional teams where you will not necessarily have direct control.

Stop and reflect on how well you are leading the innovation team and look for ways you could improve. Think about how well the team is performing and where the team is in the 'forming to mourning' model. What groups affected by the change are not in the 'committed' section of the DREC model?

What should we do?	What actions do we need to take to build the team?
Who do we need to involve?	Who needs to be involved and why?
What resources will we require?	What level of investment would be required?
What is the timing?	What deadlines do we need to meet?

Visit **www.Fast-Track-Me.com** to use the Fast Track online planning tool.

The sourcing of new knowledge for strategy making – tapping into the best brains

Dr Rebecca Steliaros

Universities are important sources of cutting-edge knowledge and skills and are increasingly important to the economic development of many mature and emerging economies. For many high-tech organisations they represent the primary source of high-quality research and other staff. But all organisations need to give consideration to where the next set of ideas will come from which might disrupt their sector.

In today's fast-moving, highly competitive business world the nature of links to universities is changing. The drivers are not cost or speed; instead companies are trying to do something different, something that they cannot do alone. Partnering with universities builds links into a global network of cutting-edge research and therefore should be thought of as long-term relationship development rather than on a case-by-case transactional basis. Most markets now move so quickly that the motivation for linking to universities is to raise the level of firm knowledge (leading to increased innovation by the firm) and find the best staff.[3] Occasionally, and particularly in lower turbulence markets, individual one-off collaborations may be set up to contribute directly to new products, but short-term projects are unlikely to reap the potential offered by a real partnership (see figure overleaf).

To get the most out of any interaction the firm first needs to have a strong internal research capacity[4] so that the results and exploitation routes through to customer value are well understood.

The most important consideration in maximising the value from interaction is building the relationship. Whilst many academics are keen to collaborate with business, most can survive without funding from this source, and unless the relationship develops to the advantage of both parties, malcontent can spread, harming a firm's chances of working with the best minds in the field again. In developing partnerships the objectives are to build strong relationships by ensuring win-win projects which fully

[3] Steliaros, R. (2008), *Knowledge Exchange Strategies in a Changing Industrial R&D Context*, MBA dissertation, Henley Business School.
[4] Martin, B., Salter, A., Hicks, D., Pavitt, K., Senker, J., Sharp, M. and von Tunzelmann, N. (1996), *The Relationship Between Publicly Funded Basic Research and Economic Performance*, a SPRU report for HM Treasury.

LONG-TERM VERSUS SHORT-TERM RELATIONSHIPS WITH UNIVERSITIES

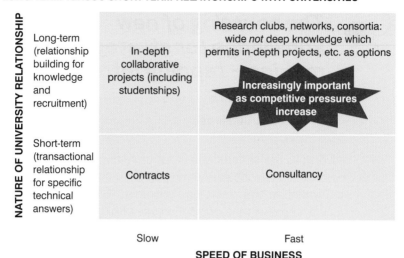

SOURCE: STELIAROS, 2008

integrate company people; and ensuring that all benefit by respecting academic drivers such as publications, students trained in a high-quality, cutting-edge research environment, etc. If this philosophy is utilised, the partners are better motivated to deliver against real needs and everyone gains.

Two key areas are critical to productive relationships:

1 **Personalities**. Can you get on with this group/person; are they interested in doing a good project (rather than money); are they likely to be responsive to your needs; is their group vibrant and do they understand the bigger picture? You are not necessarily looking for the 'best' by conventional academic metrics. Seek out intermediaries, such as government-funded organisations, that can help you find the most appropriate partners.

2 **Procedures**. Put in place project management and review steps appropriate for the magnitude of the project. Make sure the plan is flexible so that more productive unexpected avenues can be pursued; think about activities to develop their understanding of you and vice versa. For portfolios of projects ensure that selection/investment criteria are applied and think very carefully about how project outcomes will be transferred internally.

As part of the formal set-up, agreement will need to be reached over any resultant intellectual property. Strong relationships make it easier to arrive at a win-win agreement, as do open attitudes and fairness.

Linking the culture within your organisation with that of academia can seem challenging, but the opportunity to be networked into an extended, global knowledge pool and cutting-edge research can vastly accelerate innovation in your firm and result in business advantage. Ensure that you proactively manage your network for maximum benefit.

EXPERT VOICE

8

GETTING TO THE TOP

Finally, think about what you need to do to stand out amongst your peers, stay up to date and then to get ahead. As you progress up the corporate ladder you need to focus continuously on performance and increasingly look up and out as opposed to in and down. Your personal network will be more and more important and you will need to start to think and act like a director.

Focus on performance

Fast Track managers know what is important and what is not, and they focus on the key performance indicators (KPIs) that have the greatest impact on what they are trying to achieve. At all times they will understand where they are now, what the bottlenecks are and how to clear them. They regularly take time to look around for best practice, to reflect on the past in order to learn from what went well or what could be improved, and to think ahead to the future so that concerns can be resolved before they become crises. By always delivering against expectations, they stand out from the pack and will be automatic considerations for promotion at the appropriate time.

Performance snapshot: past – historic

There is a universal complaint from historians that politicians don't learn from the lessons of history. This tends to be true of businesses as well. Without a clear understanding of what has happened before, we risk repeating mistakes from the past, or reacting to a crisis that doesn't actually exist – fixing what's not broken. There was an engineering company, for example, with a poor record for delivering on time and within budget. Its poor past performance may have been undesirable, but the complete lack of competition meant that it was not in crisis; it could improve performance over time without the extra costs involved in treating the situation as a crisis.

So, review your innovation KPIs and assess how well you performed in the last period, what the trend was and perhaps what the specific problems were. This goes into the information pot for the next version of the plan.

Many organisations maintain a lessons-learned database but then rarely use it. The trouble is that a database is easy to set up but difficult for the people who you want to see them to access. After all, such a database is an important commercially sensitive asset. Think about how you in your situation will find out about what has happened before.

For example, during a project management training session in a large manufacturing company, the participants were asked how they ensured they learned from previous mistakes. They stated that it took them two days to identify databases that might contain useful information and another two days to get security clearance to look at the data, and even then the data was unstructured and next to useless. Once the manager had left the room, they all admitted that they just didn't bother any more and started with a blank piece of paper.

Performance snapshot: present – current situation (gap)

The organisation's innovation champions have to focus on the right priorities. If they don't, then they risk turning a problem into a crisis. They will want to know:

→ what is currently going on – what innovation projects are underway;

→ whether or not they are on track;

→ if not, what are the issues and who is dealing with them?

They want this information in a specific way, not as a series of vague intentions. They might use the SMART acronym by saying they want information on innovation projects that is specific, measurable, accurate, relevant and timely.

Performance snapshot: future – predictive

KPIs tend to focus on what has happened historically (just as a profit and loss account will tell you how the business performed in the last reporting period). Check that your innovation KPIs are looking in all three directions – current and future as well as past. You will want to be sure that your pipeline of ideas is still aligned to the current business imperatives, as these will often change throughout the year.

Think about risks and risk management. Constantly reassess which projects are likely to fail so that you can be ready to deal with the casualties – both the projects and the people working on them.

For example, a phone company undertook many development projects within a year in order to exploit new technologies and to stay ahead of the competition. When asked whether they were concerned about failed projects, the CEO answered that he expected at least 50 per cent of projects to fail on the basis that if they did not, they were probably not being innovative enough as an organisation. He then said that a key skill of the company's project managers was looking after the team, helping highly skilled people to come to terms with the fact that a project they had invested up to 18 months of their lives in was 'killed off'.

In summary, think ahead, plan ahead and stay ahead.

Invite challenge

Who can we get to challenge us?

Fast Track managers never rest on their laurels. You may think that your performance is on track, but as the external business environment changes you need to adapt. Look for ways to introduce challenge to you and your team on a regular basis, aiming to bring in ideas, tools and techniques from recognised innovation leaders. Review different groups:

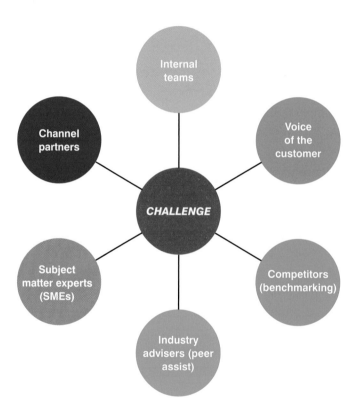

→ **Other internal teams.** What ideas can be shared? What common risks can be avoided?

→ **Customers.** How are their must-haves, needs and wants changing? What future scenarios might occur?

→ **Competitors**. What are they doing now that could be copied ('swiped' or reverse engineered)?

→ **Supply chain**. What possibilities are there for improved effectiveness and efficiency?

→ **Partners**. What can we learn from them? What opportunities are there for collaboration?

→ **Industry advisers**. What are the experts recommending? What breakthrough tools and techniques have they developed?

Engage in challenging acts on a regular basis, even if you don't need to in order to meet your KPIs because you're ahead of the game. If you are finding it easy to meet the targets set for you then don't wait for your boss to make them more stretching, do it yourself. Perhaps take time to get involved in areas where you are not confident in order to continuously develop yourself.

Remember to use relevant opportunities for self-development both inside and outside work, within your function and without. Consider the following:

→ Get involved in public speaking, such as working on internal management development courses.

→ Commission external studies, such as using undergraduate students.

→ Get involved in an outside body involved with strategic issues relating to innovation.

→ Get on to the steering committee for a professional institute.

→ Respond to public enquires (from the government) and try to get on review bodies by developing a reputation.

→ Get experience of board work through acting in the role in a company spin-out or increase your exposure to your own company board and their way of thinking by making presentations when the opportunity arises.

→ Get on internal working parties investigating company issues but possibly outside the innovation project area.

How do I keep up to date?

As well as working with other groups inside and outside the business, think carefully about what additional sources of knowledge and insight you want to receive and how often. There is a wealth of information available from a variety of sources, so you need to be selective, as the time you have available for reading is limited and the quality can be variable.

→ **Web**. This provides freely available information from a variety of sources, but is typically unstructured and will contain bias. *Fast Track recommendation: review the websites of your 'top ten' customers and competitors twice a year and identify up to five other useful websites that provide challenge.*

→ **Journals or trade magazines**. These are available via a subscription and will make the latest ideas and thinking available but will often contain a lot of commercial advertorials. *Fast Track recommendation: subscribe to the one journal of greatest relevance to your industry for one year and review its value. Once you have read it, make sure you circulate it to other members of your team.*

→ **Conferences and exhibitions**. These provide a useful opportunity to listen to stimulating presentations and are typically an excellent way of networking with others outside the business, but they can be time consuming and expensive. *Fast Track recommendation: identify the one conference of greatest relevance to your industry and attend it for two consecutive years. Aim to identify at least three people (other attendees or presenters) to follow up with about specific issues you have.*

→ **Communities of practice**. These are online discussion forums between like-minded people within the innovation community. *Fast Track recommendation: these can be extremely useful or a complete waste of time, so give them a go and see what value you get. You may also want to consider forming your own forum, but recognise that you will need to put in the necessary time and effort to get it off the ground.*

→ **Benchmarking**. This is perhaps the most valuable way of identifying new ideas and stretching the way you think, but it takes
a certain amount of effort to set up and manage. *Fast Track
recommendation: definitely worth doing, so identify two or three
other organisations who you respect as being innovative and
meet with them up to four times a year, making sure you use a
facilitator and follow a structured agenda to maximise the cross-
company learning. Remember that you will have to give value to
them as well as the other way round.*

→ **Professional bodies**. Membership of these bodies becomes
more important the more senior you become and these bodies
are often a source of free advice. *Fast Track recommendation:
once you have been in your role for at least a year, sign up for
an initial trial period and see what benefits you receive.*

→ **Fast-Track-Me.com**. All the key ideas, tools and techniques
contained in the Fast Track series are available via the internet
at **www.Fast-Track-Me.com**. *Fast Track recommendation:
firstly, allocate 30 minutes to visit and explore the site. It con-
tains a rich source of tips, tools and techniques, stories, expert
voices and online audits from the Fast Track series.*

Remember that whatever your source of information, to maximise the
benefits you need to put time aside and make the necessary effort.
However, also recognise that you will never have perfect knowledge –
particularly in the area of innovation. Take time to develop your skills in
assessing the validity and reliability of the information you have, then
decide what level of certainty will be good enough and act on it.
Remember, as the figure overleaf shows, seeking information and
removing uncertainties becomes more expensive until, for example, the
last 2 per cent is prohibitively expensive. The dangerous area in the
middle highlights the risk of making important decisions on limited information – a SWAG (sophisticated wide-arsed guess)!

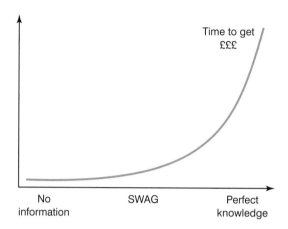

Getting promoted

At the appropriate time the Fast Track manager will seek promotion again. This may occur within a few months or possibly a number of years, but in either case take time to reflect on your state of readiness. Identify the future role you are keen to fulfil, clarify the criteria you will need to satisfy in terms of skills, experience, attitudes and behaviours, and consider how you will visibly demonstrate these attributes to others. Ask yourself the following questions.

→ **Capability**. Do I have what it takes in terms of what I have achieved and learned so far?

→ **Credibility**. Can I convince others that I can and will perform the role well?

→ **Desire**. Do I want the role and do I have sufficient drive and enthusiasm to do a great job?

→ **Relationships**. Do I have positive working relationships with the right people?

→ **Competitive**. Am I the most appropriate candidate, given the internal and external alternatives?

If you have concerns, then put in place a plan to address them. Timing will be key so make sure you are well prepared before putting yourself forward for the role. Learn how to package yourself by seeking advice and gaining feedback.

Becoming a director

 ## CASE STORY *POWERGRIND, ANDY'S STORY*

Narrator Andy was the newly appointed director of sales and marketing activities at a time when Powergrind was seeking to introduce best practice to enable it to achieve growth.

Context In the late 1980s, Powergrind was a successful manufacturer of processing machinery for the glass trade. It had grown rapidly in a market that was mature yet still fragmented. Its success came through the design, manufacture and sale of machines to cut, drill and wash glass in the UK double-glazing industry.

Issue Andy remembers his first board meeting well. There was a lot of debate around a recent internal report that confirmed that all products went out of the door late, over budget and did not meet the customer specification. Of greater concern, however, was that whilst it was recognised that this was not a recipe for long-term success, the rest of the board appeared relatively unconcerned. It's always hard to persuade a board to think about radical change when they are doing well and producing good financial results. The trouble was that if they did nothing sales would drop over a cliff.

Solution Like of a lot of companies of that time, Powergrind had grown on the back of one truly innovative product. Fortunately, during a chat with the chief executive after the meeting, Andy was somewhat relieved to learn that he accepted that one great product was not going to sustain the company in the long term and that it needed new sources of inspiration. He realised that such inspiration was not going to come from within.

Learning Andy then turned to two external sources of input. Firstly, he worked with a business school to introduce best practice – a big stretch for a company that had 'no practice' to speak of. Perhaps more significantly, he spent time listening to customers in a market where the company had no market share at all (Australia). The insights he picked up in the first two customer meetings were enough to transform the product range and enable the company to start delivering on time and within budget.

What is the role of a director?

Few organisations have the formal title of innovation director, but most will have a member of the executive team committed to driving innovation forward. In some organisations this will be the marketing director, in others it will be the R&D director or director of operations. Whatever the title, the senior innovation manager will fulfil various roles in addition to meeting statutory responsibilities, including:

→ setting the overall innovation strategy and gaining the active support of the chief executive and other members of the board;

→ championing innovation so that sufficient budget and resources are assigned to innovation activities across the organisation in the face of competition from operating divisions and other functions;

→ ensuring members of the board are aware of critical trends in the technology and the marketplace, the possible impact of each on business performance and the implications in terms of driving fundamental change;

→ designing the overall innovation framework and putting in place the appropriate teams and innovation champions to ensure effective implementation;

→ reporting on innovation progress and performance to the board, conducting stakeholder presentations and briefing key opinion leaders inside and outside the organisation.

What statutory responsibilities are there?

As well as heading up the innovation activities throughout the business, you will have certain roles and statutory responsibilities that accompany the title of director. As a member of the board of directors, you will be responsible to the shareholders of the company and be involved in:

→ determining the company's strategic objectives and policies;

→ monitoring progress towards achieving the objectives and policies;

→ appointing the senior management team;

→ accounting for the company's activities to relevant parties, e.g. shareholders;

→ ensuring that the company meets regulatory requirements, environmental standards and corporate social responsibilities (CSR);

→ attending board meetings that run the company with the high level of integrity that is inferred by statutory standards and the company's interpretation of corporate governance, particularly in sensitive areas such as health and safety.

You will also have to conduct yourself in a highly professional manner.

→ A director must not put themselves in a position where the interests of the company conflict with their personal interest or their duty to a third party.

→ A director must not make a personal profit out of their position as a director unless they are permitted to do so by the company.

→ A director must act bona fide in what they consider is in the interests of the company as a whole and not for any other purpose and with no other agenda.

How do I get to the top?

Ask yourself, 'Do I really want to get to the top?' In our early careers we often believe that this should be our natural goal, but for many people the price is too high. Whilst the personal and financial rewards can be high, many people do not enjoy the additional responsibilities, stress and pressures on the work–life balance that is often associated with getting to the top.

For one successful innovation champion, for example, an annual review with his boss was clearly not going well. Whilst he had met all his targets, his boss was telling him what he now needed to do was to get himself ready for his next promotion. After a very difficult 30-minute discussion his boss simply asked him, 'Look, don't you want to get promoted?' This was followed by silence – he had never actually thought about it in this rather stark way. After some thought, he simply replied, 'No!' He enjoyed running the workshops and getting involved with the creative idea generation and really did not want to get involved in the planning side.

Ask yourself a couple of simple questions:

→ Can I think and act strategically having spent my career to date in operational roles?

→ Do I understand other functions sufficiently to be able to integrate innovation activities?

Take time to get to know the innovation director (or director of NPD, operations or marketing). What do they do on a day-to-day basis and what do they need to achieve for success? What are the pressures and the risks? Recognise that the more senior you get, the more lonely the position is, as you end up with fewer and fewer peers. It is often said that the role of the chief executive is the loneliest one in the business.

But getting to the top in innovation is one of the most rewarding and enjoyable jobs of the lot, so if you want it go for it. Make sure you understand what criteria senior managers use to assess potential candidates for the job and seek the opportunity to work-shadow the current incumbent. Don't leave this too late as it may take you two years or more to acquire the necessary experience and skills.

Planning your exit strategy

At some stage you will want to change role. You may be moving into a different function, getting your boss's job or simply retiring, but whatever the situation the way you manage the transition is critical to sustaining the performance of your team. This is particularly important if you are considering taking members of your team with you. Take time to plan the last ten weeks in your current role to the same level of detail as you did the first ten weeks, ensuring that your successor is well prepared and excited about taking on their new role.

What is succession planning?

As soon as you have successfully completed your first ten weeks you should start to think about who will be your natural replacement. You may want to identify two or three alternatives per role, and remember that it may take at least two years to develop their skills and experience. There may be more than one internal candidate or it may be that none will meet the criteria, but in either case your succession is important and you need to plan it in advance.

Handover tips

At the point of transition, manage the handover to your successor effectively, ensuring that you transfer knowledge (both explicit and implicit) and relationships smoothly. Use the checklist in Chapter 6 (page 110) as a structure for preparing your handover document. Then focus on people and key relationships, taking time to introduce your successor face to face rather than simply sending around an email. Take time to reflect on your original vision and how well you achieved it, then capture a list of lessons learned and add it to your handover notes.

STOP – THINK – ACT

In this final chapter you will have identified what you need to do to get to the top in your chosen career. Your company may not have an innovation director per se, but innovation is likely to be a key focus within the board of directors. Stop and reflect on your career aspirations – what do you want to be doing in three years' time?

My vision	What do I want to be doing in three years' time?
My supporters	Whose support will I need to get there?
My capabilities	What capabilities and experience will I need to succeed?
My progress	What milestones will I achieve along the way?

Visit www.Fast-Track-Me.com to use the Fast Track online planning tool.

Innovation through design

Associate Professor Josiena Gotzsch

*It comes as a boom … The moment your customer realises
your idea is a great one. One they can not live without. These are
moments that make markets, destroy competition. At the heart of
that moment is a meaningful idea, the result of an insane research to
understand the customer, company and brand. Creating new opportunities.*
(ZIBA, design consultancy)

Innovation through design

Good design gives a competitive edge, specifically in mature and aggressive markets. Good design goes far beyond functionality and price and is based on multiple characteristics bringing product attraction. Additional to being functional, competitive products need to be pleasing for aesthetic, ergonomic, emotional and symbolic reasons (see figure opposite). Retro designs (bringing positive memories), elegant technological designs (reflecting on the user as an intelligent person) or environmentally friendly products (bringing a positive feeling and representing the user as a responsible person) are some examples of emotional product charisma.

Newness and surprise elements in a product concept are particularly powerful for product appeal. Newness and originality require a process of continuous innovation, an organisation that puts design at a strategic level and that is focused on bringing excellence to its client.

Implications for organisations

Design innovation is an innovation that comes from the 'outside in'. It is a creative response to a (hidden) need of the world 'outside' the company. Hardly ever is this need clearly visible. This means companies need to thoroughly understand users and increasingly seek advice from specialists such as psychologists, sociologists, anthropologists and trend analysts. Product designers are also needed. Often designers will try to understand why a product or a system is not working and use creative problem-solving skills to resolve this.

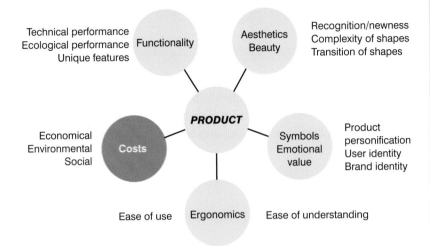

PRODUCT CHARISMA, BASED ON MULTIPLE PRODUCT CHARACTERISTICS

PRODUCT'S FUNCTIONAL VALUE *PRODUCT'S COMMUNICATIVE VALUE*

Technical performance
Ecological performance — **Functionality**
Unique features

Aesthetics
Beauty — Recognition/newness
Complexity of shapes
Transition of shapes

PRODUCT

Economical
Environmental — **Costs**
Social

Symbols
Emotional
value — Product personification
User identity
Brand identity

Ease of use — **Ergonomics** — Ease of understanding

EXPERT VOICE

To benefit most from design, the organisational structure needs to value design innovation and needs the open-mindedness and creative spirit to absorb new ideas. It means being 'streetwise', creative, playful, able to understand weak signals and having the courage to differentiate from competition. Some call this mindset 'design thinking' and companies capable of dealing with this are said to have a 'design DNA'.

When, for example, Apple developed the flattest portable computer of its time, the MacBook Air, the company aimed to add additional appeal to the technology, knowing that 'slim is in' in iPods and in multiple other electronic devices, such as portable phones, electronic photo cameras and flat screen TVs. As a result of this search for miniaturisation, Apple's R&D and that of its suppliers struggled to fit all the components into the computer. This type of development will only happen in organisations when the design function is placed in a powerful position and when its top management makes clear that this is the path to follow.

So innovation can come about through means other than traditional R&D and process improvement, by thoroughly understanding users and the companies' brand values. This is what ZIBA calls 'insane research to understand the customer, company and brand'. And then, consequently, these insights are used in the most creative manner by an organisation having the DNA, to turn these opportunities into new competitive products.

PART D

DIRECTOR'S
TOOLKIT

In Part B we introduced ten core tools and techniques that can be used from day one in your new role as a team leader or manager in your chosen field. As you progress up the career ladder to the role of senior manager, and as your team matures in terms of their understanding and capabilities, you will want to introduce more advanced or sophisticated techniques.

Part D provides a number of more advanced techniques[1] developed and adopted by industry leaders – helping you to differentiate from your competitors.

	TOOL DESCRIPTION
T1	Team innovation audit
T2	Integrated innovation framework
T3	Market and competitor scanning
T4	Creativity techniques
T5	Innovation project checklist

[1] All tools and techniques are available online at **www.Fast-Track-Me.com**

T1 TEAM INNOVATION AUDIT

Use the following checklist[1] to assess the current state of your team. Consider each criterion in turn and use the following scoring system to identify current performance:

0 Not done or defined within the business: unaware of its importance to innovation management

1 Aware of area but little or no work done in the business

2 Recognised as an area of importance and some work done in this area

3 Area clearly defined and work done in the area in terms of innovation management

4 Consistent use of best practice tools and techniques in this area across the business

5 Area is recognised as being 'best in class' and could be a reference area for best practice

Reflect on the lowest scores and identify those areas that are critical to success and flag them as status Red, requiring immediate attention. Then identify those areas that you are concerned about, and flag those as status Amber, implying areas of risk that need to be monitored closely. Status Green implies you are happy with the current state.

[1] Table on pp. 160–3 from Integrated Innovation Framework, Project Leaders International, 2008: **www.project-leaders.net**. Reprinted with permission.

ID	CATEGORY	EVALUATION CRITERIA	SCORE	STATUS
I1	Planning – Leadership		0–5	RAG
A	Strategic priority	Innovation is a strategic priority within the business and the senior management team shows active and visible commitment	☐	☐
B	Innovation executive	A member of the executive team has responsibility for the effective and efficient introduction of innovation across the business	☐	☐
C	Manager cascade	Innovation KPIs are cascaded down through the organisation so that all managers have innovation as part of their annual objectives	☐	☐
I2	Planning – Strategic focus			
A	Clear extent and direction	The organisation understands how important innovation is and the extent and direction of innovation has been defined and agreed	☐	☐
B	Customer focus	Innovation activities go beyond new product development (NPD), and embraces new markets, process re-engineering, supply chain redesign and business transformation	☐	☐
C	Integrated approach	The business has a sustainable approach to innovation across *all* functions (beyond marketing) and teams, driven by the future needs of customer musts and wants	☐	☐
I3	Pipeline – Internal sources			
A	Central database	New ideas arising from operations are captured and fed into a central decision-making forum for review (by the innovation board)	☐	☐
B	Time and budget	There is sufficient time and budget allocated to the internal generation of new ideas within formal workshops and during day-to-day activities	☐	☐
C	Breakthrough	Internal teams constantly seek ways of improving what they do and how they do it and achieving a breakthrough change in performance levels	☐	☐

ID	CATEGORY	EVALUATION CRITERIA	SCORE	STATUS
I4	Pipeline – External sources		0–5	RAG
A	Market and customer trends	Changes and discontinuities in the external environment and customer musts and wants are used to stimulate ideas for dramatic improvement in internal performance	☐	☐
B	Competitor analysis	Major customers and competitors are understood and their relative strengths and weaknesses identified – providing a rich source of new ideas that improve competitive performance	☐	☐
C	Scanning	There is a systematic approach to scanning the external and competitive environments and circulation of key insights, opportunities and threats internally across the business	☐	☐
I5	Process – Idea evaluation			
A	End-to-end process	The business has an effective and efficient 'end-to-end' innovation process (from idea to implementation) that is understood by all teams	☐	☐
A	Aligned with goals	Innovation projects are clearly aligned to strategic priorities in terms of high growth and high emphasis products and markets	☐	☐
C	Effective prioritisation	There is an effective screening and prioritisation process for ideas and innovations based on more than gut feel or who shouts the loudest	☐	☐
I6	Process – Projects and gating			
A	Best practice	Best practice innovation techniques have been defined and adopted across the business, and there is a gating process where Go/No Go decisions are made and communicated	☐	☐
B	Resources and budgets	Sufficient resources and budget are allocated to innovation projects to maximise the probability of success – implementation activities are not thrown on top of the day-job	☐	☐

ID	CATEGORY	EVALUATION CRITERIA	SCORE	STATUS
I6	Process – Projects and gating (contd)		0–5	RAG
C	Issues and risk management	Issues and risks are proactively identified, assessed and mitigated before they become crises		
I7	Platform – Support systems			
A	Full visibility and control	The senior management team has full visibility and control of the innovation process anywhere, anytime		
B	Common tool set	The system enables the consistent use of best practice techniques across the whole business including remote teams		
C	Learning culture	IT systems enable a continuous learning culture and effective knowledge management		
I8	People – Innovation champions			
A	Formal roles	The role of the innovation champion (whether full- or part-time) has been defined and exists in all critical functions		
B	Owned at all levels	The innovation process is owned at all levels (through innovation champions, chief innovation officer, project or programme manager)		
C	Right skills	Staff and management involved in innovation management have the right skills – e.g. creativity, process, project and risk management		
I9	People – Culture			
A	Supportive culture	There is a culture and system that supports continuous innovation and improvement		
B	Acceptance of failure	Whilst successes are celebrated, failures are also accepted as a possible outcome of truly innovative activities		
C	Performance system	There is a reward and recognition system (not financially based) that encourages people to identify and put forward new ideas		

ID	CATEGORY	EVALUATION CRITERIA	SCORE	STATUS
I10	Performance management		0–5	RAG
A	Agreed key performance indicators	Each innovation project has clear and agreed key performance indicators (KPIs) and return on innovation investment (ROII) targets	☐	☐
B	Clear review process	A review process for monitoring progress exists where key stakeholders will meet to review the innovation portfolio as a whole	☐	☐
C	Learning	Insights and lessons learned are captured and fed into future teams in order to maximise innovation effectiveness and avoid repeat mistakes	☐	☐

For each element of the checklist add up the scores of the three related questions and divide by 3 – this will give you an average score for that specific element. Here is an example:

ELEMENT	SCORE	0	1	2	3	4	5	NOTES
Leadership	2.1			▨				No clear strategy
Strategic focus	4.2					▨		
Internal sources	3.6				▨			Not enough people involved
External sources	4.6						▨	
Idea evaluation	1.7		▩					Paper based and inconsistent
Projects	2.6			▨				
Support systems	1.2		▩					
Innovation champions	4.6						▨	
Culture	4.4					▨		
Performance management	3.8				▨			No reward system

In your innovation framework, the whole innovation process is only as good as each individual element. If one 'link in the chain' is weak then the innovation process within the company will not operate to optimum efficiency and there is an increased risk of failure. The action plan, therefore, should be to focus attention and resources on the elements of greatest weakness first, and then to move the whole framework to a level of excellence. This approach optimises the use of resources and sets up a process of continuous improvement.

In the example above, the managers conducting the innovation audit have identified that the weakest link is that of the *support systems* used (average score 1.2). The plan would therefore be to focus attention on and improve these first until they were no longer the weakest link. Once the senior management team has increased confidence that the support systems (in this example) have improved, the next stage would be to focus on the *idea evaluation* (1.7) and *leadership* (2.1) areas.

T2 INTEGRATED INNOVATION FRAMEWORK

Why might a framework be useful?

The most effective teams identify and implement best practices – tools and techniques that the best companies use, adapted to suit their local business context. Without a framework for innovation, individuals will do their own thing their own way, and activities will be disjointed or lack efficiency and effectiveness. Another issue arising from the lack of a framework is that different managers will use different ways of setting priority for new ideas – often defaulting to who is the most senior or who shouts the loudest, as opposed to what offers the most potential benefit to the organisation.

As well as improving the effectiveness of innovation, the framework should deliver three primary objectives for the innovation champion:

→ visibility and control over the portfolio of new ideas and innovation projects, and confidence that we are focusing on the right ideas in the right priority;

→ consistent application of the agreed way of working by all teams in the business – taking innovative concepts from idea to implementation;

→ a culture of innovation and continuous improvement that embeds a learning culture.

Why does it need to be integrated?

Since innovation is vital, so is taking an integrated approach to its management. A clear business strategy that integrates innovation appropriately at its heart, combined with effective and efficient operations which allow innovation to flourish, will stand a greater chance of succeeding (see figure). The alternative is a piecemeal approach with much less chance of generating the returns expected and required by businesses.

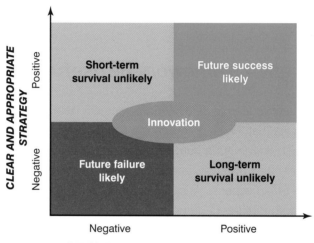

EFFECTIVE AND EFFICIENT OPERATIONS

An integrated approach means that someone should take responsibility for the innovation process within an organisation. In the last two decades we have seen the growth in numbers of chief information officers (CIOs) within large organisations charged with managing and controlling the multiplicity of systems and software that businesses use. The role is seen as core to how a business functions and operates and is represented on the board. In the same way, in the twenty-first century with its global economy, there should be a chief innovation officer or director of ideas to lead, champion and manage the innovations process. For large organisations this would be one indicator of whether a business is truly innovative and has an innovation culture.

For other organisations, how will you check whether you are truly encouraging innovations and that your organisation is getting the benefits of an innovation process? Only by using tools and techniques and by continuous monitoring of inputs and outputs to the innovation process will management understand the benefits. With so many variables, and with innovation touching every part of the business, you can only achieve this through the use of an innovation framework that stretches beyond new product development into every corner of the organisation.

An integrated innovation framework

Start by reflecting on why innovation is so necessary for survival. Most businesses can no longer compete on price alone. The costs of doing business in the UK, especially in the manufacturing sector, are far greater than those in Eastern Europe and the Far East. Reduced transportation and logistics costs and enhanced internet communications allow new and emerging competitors to compete in global markets in a way not seen by previous generations of managers. This leads to one conclusion: 'If you can't compete on price you have to differentiate, and to differentiate you have to innovate!'[1]

Despite the wealth of scientific and management expertise available, many companies lag further and further behind their competition, whilst historically other organisations have been great at coming up with ideas, but not so great at exploiting them — businesspeople talk wistfully about missed opportunities. Innovation is not just about major new ideas; innovation is often about small, incremental changes to products, services and processes. It involves all managers and staff in every department. You need to plan and manage it as a core business process. You need to integrate it into the business at both strategic and operational levels. It is the core business skill and process for the twenty-first century.

[1] Bruce, A. (2007), 'Switched on to innovation', *Professional Manager*, 16(3).

Here is a diagrammatic representation of the components of an innovation framework.

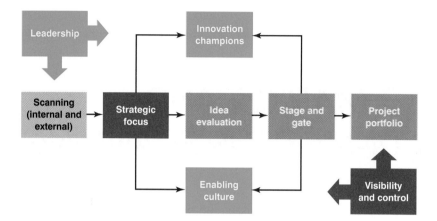

T3 MARKET AND COMPETITOR SCANNING

The importance of knowledge

Why does innovation depend on the capture of data and the accessibility of information?

At any point in time, leaders make complex choices about new ideas for improvement. This happens at all levels: from the board making a strategic decision to open up a new market, to a team leader in a call centre identifying an area of weakness in customer satisfaction. Both decisions are based on the information that provides the context within which we operate and make such decisions.

Without the facts, decision making relies too heavily on intuition or instinct, and for many of us this is not sufficient. Intuition improves with experience, and for the new manager it is all too easy to make gut-feel mistakes. Sceptical managers refer to this as SWAGging. They listen to people using lots of fancy terminology and jargon to explain why they made a particular decision whilst in reality everyone knows it was based on some good information and some that was little more that guesswork. This is referred to as a sophisticated wide-arsed guess, or SWAG! It's a bit like the mathematician who won the prize at a fair for guessing the number of beans in a huge bottle. When asked how he did it he replied, 'I used trigonometry and then allowed 45 per cent for error'.

Innovation does concern the future and that is difficult to forecast, but don't underestimate the importance of gathering data on a continuous basis and making it accessible to people engaged in innovative thinking.

So what information is required?

Innovation requires more than simply getting a group of people together in a room and asking them to think creatively. This tends to result in solutions and action plans that are essentially more of the same, although 10 per cent better. A long period of working like that could end with you being the world's most efficient manufacturer of black and white televisions.

Perhaps the introduction of good information to the process is a key distinction between innovation and continuous improvement. Continuous improvement is rather inward looking, continuously checking if we can do current things better; whilst if you stimulate creative thought and your awareness of business needs by an awareness of the outside world, you get to innovation.

The rate and extent of change going on around us and, of course, the industry and business context you are working in will to a large extent determine the requirement for information; but we can define the following categories of information as a checklist to make sure that the information-gathering phase of the process of innovation is as effective as possible.

Market scanning

Without a good understanding of what is happening in the industry or market in which we compete, we run the risk of missing exciting new markets, or failing to see threats until it is too late to respond. Trends in the external environment present both opportunities and threats, but in both cases innovative solutions are required to stay ahead. Many new ideas will originate outside the organisation. Suppliers, for example, will continuously present you with new opportunities if their innovation is keeping them ahead of the pack.

Many companies are employing the new term 'search and development' (as opposed to research and development) to make sure they identify people charged with seeing what others are doing and finding a way of doing it faster, better or cheaper.

Most organisational improvements are driven in one way or another by trends or discontinuities in the industry in which they operate. A discontinuity refers to a dramatic change in the business context, such as a breakthrough in technology from the old-style television to the use of flat screens. PESTEL (political changes, economic trends, social trends, technology discontinuities, environmental trends and legal changes) gives you a structured model to look for sources of new ideas:

Political changes

A change in government or the introduction of new policies will impact many aspects of the economy. It will also result in levels of uncertainty and make organisations more or less willing to invest in new ventures. For example:

→ **Policies on healthcare spending change with each new government.** Providers of homecare services to the elderly innovate to reduce their dependency on government contracts – effectively spreading their risk.

→ **The awarding of new mobile network licences is often essentially a political decision.** Network operators innovate to create new services to recoup their investment in this new technology as quickly as possible.

Economic trends

International exchange rates, rates of inflation or even changes in tax regimes will affect disposable incomes and therefore consumer (and business) spending. For example:

→ **In tight economic times business discretionary spend gets slashed.** Training providers are often very hard hit, and so they innovate to drive costs down and demonstrate return on investment.

→ **As interest rates come down, the cost of borrowing goes down.** Financial services organisations innovate to introduce new forms of borrowing and ways of restructuring corporate debt.

Social trends

Changes in demographics such as an ageing population, immigration and emigration or movement into or out of towns will fundamentally change patterns of buying behaviour. For example:

→ **Consumer buying habits are changing as more people are using the internet to buy online.** Traditional retailers innovate to change the way they market to and service this new segment.

→ **Improvements in healthcare have resulted in people living longer and having more active lives.** Pharmaceutical companies innovate to create new products to serve this new market segment.

Technology discontinuities

Perhaps the biggest external driver for many organisations in recent years has been the relentless developments in all aspects of technology, such as the internet and mobile telephony. For example:

→ **The internet has allowed small and medium-sized enterprises (SMEs) to compete head to head with global companies – often aggressively taking market share in the most profitable niches.** Large corporations in all sectors innovate to find ways of servicing and retaining existing customers.

→ **The power of computers and multimedia recorders has slashed the cost of replicating music and videos.** Major Hollywood studios innovate to find ways of defeating pirates.

Environmental trends

Consideration and care for the environment is getting unprecedented press at present, covering issues ranging from global warming and recycling to working with third world countries. For example:

→ **Genetically modified (GM) crops offer enormous potential to produce more for less, but future legislation is still unclear.** Farmers innovate to find ways of preparing for the introduction of GM crops without crippling current operations and revenue streams.

→ **Global warming is changing the climate in many regions of the world.** International tourism operators innovate to identify and develop new holiday destinations.

Legal changes

Most Western organisations complain bitterly of the increasing number of laws and regulations they need to comply with. Following recent corporate failures, new standards are being adopted, such as Sarbanes-Oxley. This is a new standard for monitoring and reporting on the business that arose out of corporate failures in the US, but ultimately impacted all European companies dealing with American companies. For example:

→ **New European laws affect all companies operating within the region.** New member states innovate to ensure their products and services comply with standards so that they can be sold in what is a new market for them.

→ **Compliance with new standards adds considerably to costs at a time when most organisations are under relentless cost pressures.** Financial services organisations innovate to introduce new processes that ensure compliance whilst minimising overhead and bureaucracy.

Competitor scanning

Without a good understanding of customers and competitors we run the risk of producing products and services that simply will not sell, either because customers don't want them or because they can get them better, cheaper, faster elsewhere. Remember what is important when gathering information about customers and competitors. You need to know what you are offering to your customers and, more importantly, their perception of what you are offering them. The same with competitors: find out how their customers perceive their products and services as well as what they actually are. The 'So what?' test is useful here. If a competitor has a feature that you do not have, make sure it is significant either to their market share or to their customer satisfaction score before taking it as a must-have for your product. Similarly, don't let the fact that you have a unique feature make you think that you automatically have a competitive advantage. Look for information that tells you that customers will want such a feature in the future.

Gather data in three areas: customers, competitors and substitutes and alternatives.

Customers

Changes in customer must-haves and wants will fundamentally change what it is we do or how we do it: so we need to listen to them and get their feedback. But this is more difficult than it looks since customer satisfaction surveys are not necessarily good predictors of future purchasing behaviours. Too often companies score 9 out of 10 on a survey and then lose the next contract because of a change in the customer environment that has altered customers' requirements. You are gathering data about the future, not just about the past.

We need to understand how customers' requirements are changing, what is now most important to them and what their biggest concerns are. Then we can innovate around how we can use our capabilities to provide exciting new solutions. For example:

→ Using a focus group to conduct market research, a bank identified a group of customers that were increasingly comfortable with new technologies. This trend led to the launch of First Direct, a telephone and internet-based bank.

→ Sitting down and listening to its top ten customers, Machinery Manufacturer Powergrind redesigned the whole of its engineering product line to incorporate new technologies to allow self-diagnosis of problems by customers.

Competitors

When looking at customer must-haves and wants it is not enough to understand how we perform. We need to identify how we perform against the competition – what are our strengths and weaknesses? Where have we got an advantage that we can exploit and where have we got weaknesses that we need to address?

Analysis of competitors' needs to be more than a simple cursory review of their financials (balance sheets and profit and loss statements). Think about: background information; what products and services they offer and to which customers and markets; what facilities they have; and how large their team is. Perhaps of most interest to your innovation team is to try to predict what their future strategies will be and, therefore, where you may need to innovate to protect any current advantages you may have.

Consider using a structured approach to the analysis of competitors:

- 1
  - Define, scope and segment the industry you are in
  - Include size, growth and maturity

- 2
  - Determine major customer and consumer groups
  - Identify channels to market and potential barriers to entry

- 3
  - Identify competitors (current and potential)
  - Identify substitute products and services

- 4
  - Determine key success factors (KSFs) to win future business
  - Classify customer criteria into musts and wants and then prioritise

- 5
  - Gather facts about competitors (financials, products, markets operations)
  - Validate facts and build intelligence

- 6
  - Assess competitors against market KSFs and customer musts and wants
  - Identify relative strengths and weaknesses

- 7
  - Identify specific opportunities and threats, sources of advantage and product/service unique selling propositions (USPs)

- 8
  - Plan innovation workshops to identify new ideas to exploit opportunities and address threats

Substitutes and alternatives

And you're not finished yet: start thinking outside the box. So your customers like what you are offering and your competitors appear at a disadvantage; where else might you face a threat? Well, from the blind-side actually. There are people in other industries, perhaps so different from yours that you've never even thought of them as a competitor, who may be looking at, for example, changes in technology that might just give them a new solution to your customers' problems that makes your product look expensive or out of date. For example:

→ Major airlines spent a lot of time coming up with innovative ideas for fending off the threat from American airlines and other so-called flag carriers, and completely missed the threat from new low-cost **alternatives** such as easyJet and Ryanair.

→ Similarly, when times are hard an airline knows that businesspeople will drop the class of travel they use to save money. Airlines must also be aware of possible **substitutes** for businesspeople travelling to meetings at all: the threats from the internet, from video conferencing and from mobile phones. Fundamentally, face-to-face communication is not found to be so necessary when times are hard, and technology is constantly improving its ability to simulate a one-on-one meeting.

T4 CREATIVITY TECHNIQUES

For many teams, simply having the opportunity to get together with colleagues away from day-to-day activities is enough to generate hundreds of creative ideas for performance improvement. There is no need to stimulate their creative thinking through the use of formal tools and techniques. However, there are times when selective use of methods of encouraging creativity can make a big difference:

→ Teams can quickly dry up and not enough ideas are put forward.

→ Free-form idea generation can often result in tactical solutions that fail to identify or address major business challenges.

Take time to review the creativity methods listed (and illustrated in the figure overleaf), and plan to use one or two of them at your next focused innovation workshop. However, recognise that before using any technique with a group, you should always allow time at the start to capture the ideas that people will already have thought of before coming into the session, as you will not have their full attention until they have shared them with the group.

Objects

Use a list of objects to stimulate creative ideas. The list can be drawn from objects in the room you are working in or selected at random out of a dictionary. For example, a telecoms company needed new ideas for a mobile phone and the object they started with was a 'brick'. Within two

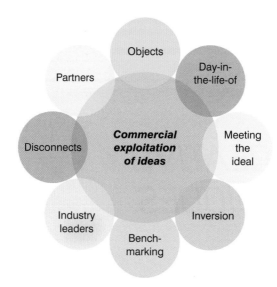

minutes they had identified 20 new ideas, including modular construction, colour covers, user assembly and rugged cases.

Day-in-the-life-of (DILO)

How well do you understand your customers and what their needs are? A DILO study maps out what a typical customer does from the time they wake up to the time they go to bed, and it explores ways in which a company's offerings could be adapted to solve other customer problems. For example, mobile phones now have alarms to wake people up and remind them of appointments. This approach will also work for different stages of a person's career or life cycle – for example, children want games on their phones.

Meeting the ideal

A simple way of improving what you offer is to break down customer expectations into a series of must and wants, and then to ask, 'What would the customer consider to be ideal performance against each criteria?' Whilst you may not be able to meet all of them, this provides an effective challenge and will nearly always stimulate different ways of working. A machinery manufacturer invested time meeting face to face with prospective customers in an overseas market and discovered that their 'ideal' was to be able to fix their machines themselves if they broke down. A ten-minute brainstorm back in the office resulted in an idea to introduce self-diagnostics into the next generation of machine. This not only transformed the export market, but also led to increased sales in the domestic market.

Inversion

Inversion encourages the team to think the opposite of their established position or thinking. This requires challenging the mindset of the team. We see a good example of this thinking in the way that computer processing power went from the mainframe to the desktop PC in the 1980s, and then with the evolution of the web, central processing is now going back to a central server.

Benchmarking

Whilst many creative ideas for improvement will come from internal teams, there are typically many things that can be learned from your most effective competitors. Make a list of your major competitors, pick one or two of them and then research what it is they do that makes them distinctive or special. However, don't necessarily look to replicate what they do, but explore what you could do that would potentially leap-frog them.

Industry leaders

A common complaint of creative ideas is that they don't necessarily deliver real value to the bottom line. To address this concern, start by making a list of the largest and most successful companies in your industry, and ask yourself how you could deliver products and services to them in a way that will impact their operating performance. After all, whilst you can be successful serving small companies in a declining market niche, it is often easier to succeed working with profitable industry leaders. Richmond Foods, the UK's largest manufacturer of ice cream, focused the majority of its innovation activities on serving the needs of Tesco, and as a result it grew dramatically on the back of Tesco's increasing dominance of the retail sector.

Disconnects

Fundamental changes in market conditions will always result in opportunities for change and innovation. Take time to scan your external and competitive environments in order to identify significant changes or discontinuities, either current or potential, and then explore ways in which you could exploit such changes. These changes may relate to new technologies, regulatory changes or new competition. Ritchey Group (now Animalcare Group), the UK's leading agricultural supplier, grew by more than 100 per cent over an 18-month period simply by monitoring new European legislation and then creating a tagging product for cattle that exploited that legislation.

Partners

Many organisations are quite blinkered in thinking they have to do everything themselves, and as a result their innovation activities can often be quite restricted. Think differently about what you do and how you do it – focusing on your core capabilities. Then explore ways in which you could work with other organisations to find creative solutions to major challenges within your industry. A good example of this is the way that major petrol companies such as Shell and BP have partnered with major retailers such as Tesco and Marks & Spencer to provide a one-stop-shop for busy executives and parents.

Finally, a word of warning

Generating new ideas will achieve little unless they are effectively screened, prioritised and actioned. Use techniques such as the V-SAFE screening funnel to focus on the right ideas and ensure the right people are involved in planning implementation actions.

T5 INNOVATION PROJECT CHECKLIST

What process can we follow to implement ideas?

There is no one right or wrong answer to this, and the stages and gates will vary enormously depending on the industry, the size of the business or the complexity of the project. Some new ideas can be implemented quickly and simply: for example, radically changing the pricing policy could possibly be achieved by one person over the period of an hour. However, if the innovative idea is to expand into Europe, then a five-minute chat over lunch is probably insufficient. Spend an appropriate amount of time planning and, where possible, use simple checklists to make sure everyone is following a common approach based on best practice.

What is a typical workplan?

The table overleaf reflects the generic tasks that would be included in each stage from developing an idea to implementation. Not all will be applicable to all projects, and many will need to be adapted to suit your business and your specific needs.

The lists are fairly comprehensive and as such look a little daunting. Go through them and decide where you need to take a shortcut or adapt the methodology to take account of your specific case and timescale constraints. Sometimes you have to go for it and leave a few stones unturned.

Reflect on each item and assess a current innovation project you are working on. Assess each activity using a simple RAG scale for status, where Red suggests major concerns and that you should take immediate corrective actions, Amber suggests some concerns and risks, and needs to be monitored closely, and Green indicates useful activity that is on track.

WORKPLAN		DESCRIPTION OF POSSIBLE ACTIVITIES	STATUS
Stage 1 Initiate			
1	Strategic priorities	Review strategic, product-market and brand imperatives to identify innovation scope, direction and product/market/ process priorities	☐
2	Market analysis	Conduct analysis to understand macro-economic trends, current and prospective customers, end-users/ consumers and key competitors. Research best practices and market leaders	☐
3	Internal audit	Conduct an internal audit of core capabilities (all aspects of the supply chain) and summarise in the form of critical strengths and weaknesses. Review the databases of internal lessons learned	☐
4	Idea generation workshop	Identify emerging opportunities and threats and collect initial ideas from primary and secondary sources. Use brainstorming techniques and other creative tools to generate ideas from the historical insights/ lessons learned and analysis. This step is sometimes referred to as 'ideation'	☐
5	Idea development	Group and sort ideas into bigger ideas – look for 'breakthroughs', look at converging and disparate ideas and conduct an initial 'refinement' of ideas	☐
6	Idea refinement	Develop the initial idea and unique selling proposition (USP), create 'story boards'/ sketches and selling proposition (ten-second elevator pitch). Develop an outline marketing flier – what would it say?	☐
7	Project charter	Initiate the formal project charter, including outline idea, outline profit and loss, potential project leader and in-market period	☐

WORKPLAN	DESCRIPTION OF POSSIBLE ACTIVITIES	STATUS

Stage 1 Initiate (contd)

8	Preliminary screen	Conduct a preliminary financial and capability screening and risk assessment. Use 'quick screening' criteria, including assessment against value contribution, strategic/brand fit, stakeholder acceptance, implementation feasibility and timescales (V-SAFE)	☐
9	Timing and dependencies	Identify preliminary timings and intra-project dependencies and explore potential critical issues/resources	☐
10	Idea approval	Complete formal idea evaluation (Go, No Go/Kill, Modify or Wait) and prepare gate documents	☐

Stage 2 Business case

1	Team initiation	Assign project leader(s) and initial members of the core team. Conduct project team kick-off workshop. Identify training needs and develop capability plans	☐
2	Concept development	Develop top-level concept (draft) and develop core creative idea. Test the concept (conduct qualitative analysis – brand positioning and target audience). Refine the concept based on test results	☐
3	Brief	Develop product or solution brief with opportunity assessment. Gain feedback from relevant functions (financial, sales and marketing, R&D, quality assurance, operations, trading, legal, market research)	☐
4	Proof of concept	Pre-prototype and conduct qualitative consumer tests (if appropriate), including user/consumer validation	☐
5	Operational impact	Conduct preliminary assessment of impact on manufacturing, operations and supply chain/route to market	☐
6	Initial financials	Agree preliminary sales/financial forecasts, market share and value (price, cost and investments), and create a multi-year forecast and preliminary return on innovation investment (including assumptions). Include portfolio assessment and potential synergy with other initiatives	☐

WORKPLAN	DESCRIPTION OF POSSIBLE ACTIVITIES	STATUS

Stage 2 Business case (contd)

7	Stakeholder buy-in	Gain stakeholder agreement to the business case, capital expenditure (CapEx), go-live activities, route to market, manufacturing and legal/claims	☐
8	Project plan	Agree initial project timetable. Develop a communication strategy/plan	☐
9	Risk assessment	Conduct formal risk assessment on project plan, assumptions and capabilities	☐
10	Product financials	Develop preliminary profit and loss (P&L) forecast with return on innovation investment (ROII) and financial payback. Finalise business case and prepare gate documents	☐

Stage 3 Develop

1	Prototype development	Create a solution prototype and validate internally. Conduct user/consumer tests (quantitative) or pilot test prototype (as appropriate)	☐
2	Product refinement	Fine-tune the solution based on user/consumer feedback (product, package, positioning, pricing, etc.) and modify as required. Conduct technical tests (and field trials if required)	☐
3	Regulatory and trademark	Gain quality, compliance, regulatory, trademark and legal clearance (internal/external)	☐
4	Final specification	Develop final solution specification and agree with key stakeholders and relevant elements of the supply chain	☐
5	Product briefs	Develop an outline communication plan based on agreed positioning and sensitivities. Develop an internal PR plan and internal sell-in pack	☐
6	Stakeholder commitment	Gain stakeholder agreement to final business case and launch plan and commitment to implementation support	☐
7	Process optimisation	Critically review opportunities for improvement in the effectiveness and efficiency of the innovation process	☐
8	Quality/compliance	Conduct quantitative test of mix and potential, conduct formal quality review and audit process, products, systems, skills and supply chain	☐

WORKPLAN	DESCRIPTION OF POSSIBLE ACTIVITIES	STATUS
Stage 3 Develop (contd)		
9 Launch plan	Develop financial plan with three-year profit and loss (P&L) forecast, develop preliminary go-live plan and communication strategy, confirm required investments	☐
10 Final business case	Finalise project budgets and timetable, and prepare gate documents	☐
Stage 4 Validate		
1 Authorisations	Obtain formal authorisations/sign-offs as required (capital, product, governance and legal/regulatory)	☐
2 Supply chain changes	Implement supply chain/logistics changes and develop production and distribution capability as required	☐
3 Marketing materials	Finalise internal and external marketing materials. Develop sales material and produce samples for sales preparation. Develop advertising material and incentives and purchase media as required	☐
4 Communication plan	Develop communication plan – what (key messages) to whom (stakeholders). Confirm key stakeholder support and clarify deliverables. Develop 'selling story' and develop support materials around the core idea	☐
5 Media strategy	Complete a detailed media strategy with question and answers (Q&As), statements and press releases including stories, reference sells and claims	☐
6 Sales presentations	Conduct sales presentations and modify materials based on initial feedback	☐
7 Pilot launch	Conduct a limited scope commercial launch to test all aspects of the solution and supply chain	☐
8 Success indicators	Identify and agree key success factors (KSFs), key performance indicators (KPIs) (initial and ongoing) and success hurdles. Update risk assessment	☐
9 Growth options	Create options and plans for ongoing user/customer support, internal solution life-cycle management and future expansion/innovation as required	☐
10 Launch plan	Complete final integrated launch plan (including qualified business case and timings) and prepare gate documents	☐

WORKPLAN	DESCRIPTION OF POSSIBLE ACTIVITIES	STATUS

Stage 5 Scale (go-to-market) or exit

1	Commercial production	Activate first commercial production/solution implementation and supply chain	☐
2	Sales and marketing	Execute communication plan, activate media launch and execute internal/external sales plan	☐
3	Post-launch sales support	Distribute marketing material and incentives, launch activation and execute marketing activities	☐
4	Monitoring and control	Monitor launch plan (completion of tasks), identify and resolve (or escalate) critical issues and risks, motivate the team (identify additional development needs) and conduct regular review meetings	☐
5	Early indicators	Conduct performance audits, track performance in market (specifically early indicators) and adjust plans as required	☐
6	Performance reviews	Review performance against success indicators (KPIs) – did the project deliver on time and within budget, and what needs to change for next time?	☐
7	Stakeholder reviews	Conduct formal close-down reviews (meetings) with key stakeholders including user/customer/consumer groups and supply chain	☐
8	Team congratulations	Congratulate and disband the team, update personal development plans (PDPs) and agree next roles	☐
9	Lessons learned	Capture and share learning and insights with other teams, update 'best practice' databases and communicate to interested parties	☐
10	Operational handover	Formerly transfer ownership and responsibility to operational teams. Scale operations as required or exit/close	☐

THE FAST TRACK WAY

Take time to reflect

Within the Fast Track series, we cover a lot of ground quickly. Depending on your current role, company or situation, some ideas will be more relevant than others. Go back to your individual and team audits and reflect on the 'gaps' you have identified, and then take time to review each of the top ten tools and techniques and list of technologies.

Next steps

Based on this review, you will identify many ideas about how to improve your performance, but look before you leap: take time to plan your next steps carefully. Rushing into action is rarely the best way to progress unless you are facing a crisis. Think carefully about your own personal career development and that of your team. Identify a starting place and consider what would have a significant impact on performance and be easy to implement. Then make a simple to-do list with timings for completion.

Staying ahead

Finally, the fact that you have taken time to read and think hard about the ideas presented here suggests that you are already a professional in your chosen discipline. However, all areas of business leadership are changing rapidly and you need to take steps to stay ahead as a leader in your field. Take time to log in to the Fast Track web-resource, at **www.Fast-Track-Me.com**, and join a community of like-minded professionals.

Good luck!

OTHER TITLES IN THE FAST TRACK SERIES

This title is one of many in the Fast Track series that you may be interested in exploring. Whilst each title works as a standalone solution, together they provide a comprehensive cross-functional approach that creates a common business language and structure. The series includes titles on the following:

→ Strategy

→ Project management

→ Finance

→ Sales

→ Marketing

GLOSSARY

adoption curve The phases through which consumers or the market as a whole move when adopting a new product or service: innovators, early adopters, early majority, late majority, laggards

alliance A formal agreement between two companies in order to develop a new product or exploit a new market where risks and rewards are shared

alpha test Testing of a new product before the production stage in order to identify and eliminate problems. These tests may use historical data and are sometimes referred to as 'dry runs'

analysis Formal evaluation of data or known facts in order to come to a conclusion

attribute testing A method of identifying customer or consumer preferences by asking them to rate a list of products or attributes using a common scale

awareness A measure of how many or what percentage of target customers are aware of a particular product or brand

balanced scorecard A group of performance indicators covering four categories:
1 financial results;
2 customer and brand;
3 operational excellence; and
4 people and learning

benchmarking A method of comparing the performance of one company or process with others, including the market leader or recognised best practice

benefit An attribute of a product or service expressed in terms of the positive impact it has on the user

best practice Processes, skills and systems that are considered to deliver optimum performance. These are often associated with market leaders

beta test Tests carried out externally in order to identify and mitigate problems prior to production. These tests should use real data and are sometimes referred to as 'wet runs'

beyond NPD An expression used to get innovation teams to think more broadly than simply the creation of new products. For example, most new ideas relate to new packaging, new operational process or innovative ways of getting the same product to market

brainstorming A method of generating new ideas around a particular topic within a group situation. The key is to make the initial list quickly without discussion before evaluating the list as a whole

brand A name, design or feature that distinguishes one product or company from another. The brand is often associated with perceptions and perceived benefits

breakthrough A fundamentally different idea or way of thinking that is clearly distinctive when compared with similar ideas

business case A formal analysis of a new idea to validate whether it will provide a satisfactory return on the investment required to make it happen

business-to-business (B2B) A term referring to commercial transactions between two organisations and not involving sales directly to consumers

[1] A comprehensive glossary of all business terms is available online at **www.Fast-Track-Me.com**

business-to-consumer (B2C) A term referring to transactions between an organisation and the consumer and not going through a third-party channel

cannibalisation The amount of demand for a new product that results from the reduction of demand for a current product or service. This has to be taken into consideration when calculating the real return on investment of a new idea

champion The person who is prepared to ensure that a new idea is implemented effectively. This person is often a senior manager with a high degree of passion or vested interest in the success of the new idea

commercialisation The process of taking a new product or service idea to a commercial market in order to gain profitable returns, typically involving sales, marketing and supply chain developments

competitive intelligence Information about competitors that enables an organisation to gain competitive advantage. For example, this may relate to their strengths and weaknesses or their plans for new product introductions

competitor analysis The formal analysis of a competitor involving the review of their financial performance, as well as their strategy, operations, product lines and customer base

concept A description of a new idea that articulates top-level features and benefits

concurrent engineering The process of implementing a new idea where various activities are conducted at the same time (or in parallel)

consumer The user of a product or service. This may or may not be the person who buys it

contingency plan A plan to mitigate the effects of a potential problem, should it occur. This is particularly useful when introducing complex

ideas or ideas that are critical to future business performance

convergent thinking A method for reducing the number of ideas or concepts down to a manageable number, possibly using structure criteria (see also V-SAFE)

core benefit proposition (CBP) The main benefit of value that customers will receive as a result of adopting a new idea

corporate culture The values, operating principles or shared beliefs within an organisation that are adhered to by people in the organisation. This is heavily influenced by the founders or the chief executive and will affect the adoption of a culture of continuous innovation

creativity The process of thinking about and generating new ideas

critical assumption An assumption made about the future that will have a significant impact on the success or failure of a new idea. Each assumption will have associated risks that should be mitigated

critical success factors (CSF) Factors of a new idea or its implementation that are necessary for successful introduction

crossing the chasm Successfully making the transition from the innovation stage of introducing a new idea to adoption by the mass market. The term 'chasm' relates to the risk of failure associated with an idea that has yet to prove its worth

customer The person who purchases a product or service

customer needs Specific problems for which a customer needs a solution

customer value analysis A structured approach to analysis of customer musts and wants, showing how a company performs against its competitors

dashboard An electronic (computer) display of information relating to the performance of a team, process, product or business

decision tree A process for making decisions where ideas (or choices) and alternative outcomes are presented in the form of branches on a tree

defensive innovation The development of new ideas (such as product line extensions) in order to protect an existing position in the market from attack by competitors

design of experiments (DOE) A method for simultaneously evaluating multiple parameters in order to identify most likely outcomes in terms of the success or failure of a new idea

development The process of taking a new product or service idea to the stage that it can be evaluated in the market

differentiation The distinct attributes or features of an idea that help to provide a source of advantage over competitors

discontinuity A major change in market conditions that creates significant opportunities and threats for all businesses operating within the market. These might relate to changes in legislation, technology or demographics

discontinuous innovation Creating and launching a completely new product, service or process improvement idea as opposed to incremental change. It often results from the adoption of a new technology or the reaction to a major market trend

divergent thinking A process to encourage more creative thinking in the early part of the overall innovation process

early adopters Customers who will use their own judgement to adopt a new product or service very early on in its life cycle

economic value add (EVA) The financial value associated with a new idea, taking into account life cycle costs and benefits

entrepreneur A person who initiates, leads, takes the risks and gets the rewards from a new venture

exit strategy A plan for withdrawing a new idea at a point in time. This might be due to a limited market or declining performance. This term also refers to a planned sale of a business by its founders

features Characteristics of an idea, product or service that provide benefits to customers or consumers

first to market The first product or service in a new emerging market. These products will often gain what is called first mover or prime mover advantage

focus group A market research method where a group of customers meet in one room to discuss the pros and cons associated with an idea

Gantt chart A plan of activities within a project presented graphically as a series of boxes against a timeline. This technique was developed by Henry Gantt as a highly effective way of communicating project plans and progress to stakeholders

gap analysis An assessment of the difference between the current performance and the desired or target performance

gate A point in the development and commercialisation of a new idea where a formal Go/No-Go decision will be made

gate keepers A group of managers and subject matter experts that will make the formal Go/No-go decision on a new idea at regular formal review points, sometimes called gates

idea A thought or concept for improving performance in terms of a new product or feature, a new market or channel, or a new way of working or business process

ideation Activities at the start of the innovation process that generate creative new ideas

incremental innovation Small improvements in performance resulting from the introduction of a new idea, similar to continuous improvement (CI)

innovation The commercial exploitation of ideas. Creativity relates to the generation of ideas, whereas the innovation process embraces implementation of those ideas within the market or business context

innovation review board A group of managers and subject matter experts that will make the formal Go/No-go decision on a new idea at regular formal review points, sometimes called gates (see also *gate keepers*)

innovation strategy A plan for the future, expressing the extent and direction of innovation: process improvement; extended or new product/service development; extended or new market/channel development; and diversification. These choices will reflect the required investment levels and the firm's attitude to risk

insight New information that is of potential value to the person who developed it, their team or their organisation

integrated product development (IPD) Development of new products or services in a way that combines inputs from a variety of functions (see also *concurrent engineering*)

intellectual property (IP) Information relating to an idea, including proprietary knowledge, designs and brands, that is formally protected by law

intrapreneur Someone who develops new enterprises within a much larger organisation. Similar to entrepreneur, but working for someone else such as a division of a large company

inversion A creativity technique that encourages a team to challenge traditional thinking. For example, computer design started with central mainframe computers and went to personal computers, and is now going back to central servers running applications over the internet

ISO-9000 An internationally recognised quality standard. This is sometimes necessary for winning contracts with public sector organisations and large corporations where demonstrable quality is required

kaizen A Japanese term meaning continuous improvement

learning organisation An organisation or team that adopts a structured approach to the capture and sharing of insights or lessons learned from operational activities such as the introduction of new products

life-cycle cost The total cost of implementing a new idea from concept and implementation to operational costs, ongoing support and any decommissioning costs

market development Activities to take an existing product or service into a new market or to grow the overall size and shape of a market

market research Analysis of a market in order to understand its various attributes in terms of size and growth, segmentation, customer-buying decision criteria and competition

market share Sales of a particular product, service or firm as a percentage of the overall market

market testing Formal evaluation of a new idea with customers, either within a controlled environment such as a focus group, or within a pilot market

marketing Activities to increase the awareness of a new idea, product or service within a target customer group

markets A collection of current or potential customers

maturity The stage of the product life cycle where there are only a few remaining prospective customers. These customers are often the most difficult ones to convince, and such a market is often very competitive

metrics Key performance indicators used to assess the value of a new idea. These should ideally be balanced in terms of financial, operational and strategic indicators

nemawashi A Japanese term meaning to 'nurture the roots' of an idea. Many ideas stand a better chance of being supported by others if the 'seeds' of the idea are planted in meetings and discussions before any formal decision point

net present value (NPV) A method of valuing a new idea that takes projected future cash flows (profits) discounted by the level of risk associated with each period. Typically the more risky an idea, the less certainty there will be with future forecasts

new business development (NBD) The process for developing a new business based on a breakthrough in thinking, technology, product functionality or market access. It is often implemented within a partnering agreement as no one organisation will have the full range of capabilities for success

new product development (NPD) The process for developing a new product from initial concept or idea to in-market commercialisation

new service development The process for developing a new service offering from initial concept or idea to in-market commercialisation

nominal group technique (NGT) A brainstorming technique in which members of a group write down their ideas individually before sharing them with others

offensive innovation The development of new ideas in order to exploit an opportunity in the market or to aggressively attack a competitor

opportunity cost Lost benefits of costs associated with the adoption of an idea. For example, developing one product may prohibit the development of an alternative product

Pareto profile A graphical representation of a series of ideas, products or markets, ordered to show those with the highest value or contribution at one end, descending to the lowest contribution. This technique is useful for getting a team to identify and focus on priorities

patents Legal protection of an idea that protects the concept or design from being copied or reverse-engineered by competitors for a period of time

peer assist Use of colleagues or subject matter experts from other departments or external organisations to critically review and challenge progress or performance

performance indicators Measures of performance associated with an idea. They should be SMART: specific to the idea, measurable, agreed, realistic and time bound

pipeline A list of future ideas for consideration or implementation

Porter's five forces An analytic framework developed by Michael Porter to analyse the current trends and drivers in an industry. Opportunities will be identified wherever there is a significant change or 'discontinuity' in the industry

portfolio A group of ideas, projects, products or markets. If they are related or have a common shared goal they would be referred to as a programme

portfolio map A graphical representation of a portfolio of ideas or projects, used to identify the relative strengths and weaknesses of each item. Axes will vary but most common will be market attractiveness and competitive position

process champion The person responsible for the design, management and continuous improvement of an operational process. Process innovation is necessary in order to improve overall effectiveness and efficiency

process map A graphical representation of a process, where the activities are linked to show the natural sequence, and are displayed against roles (known as a 'swimlane' format. Process maps are useful analytic tools for identifying opportunities for process improvement

process re-engineering A structured approach to the fundamental redesign of a process, often starting with a blank piece of paper

products Goods and services created and sold to customers

product development The process for developing a new product or service from initial concept or idea to in-market commercialisation

product life cycle The stages that a new product will go through: introduction, growth, maturity and decline. Product life-cycle management (PLM) is the process of managing the entire life cycle of a product through each of these stages

product line A group of products or services with similar characteristics or attributes, possibly sold under the same brand

project A series of activities designed to deliver a goal, with an agreed start and end point. What constitutes a project is often hotly debated, but most discrete activities within an organisation can be defined as projects

project leader/manager The person with the overall responsibility for delivery of project objectives, on time and within budget

project management The process of defining, planning, managing and controlling project activities. This will include the monitoring of performance improvement targets and the selection and motivation of the team

project plan A list of activities necessary to complete a project on time and within budget. These activities are often grouped into phases and will sometimes show ownership, timing and dependencies. Plans can also be displayed in a graphical format (see also *Gantt chart*)

project portfolio A group of ideas or projects. If they are related or have a common shared goal they would be referred to as a programme

project sponsor The member of the senior management team with responsibility for championing a project. They will set the overall objectives for the project, select the project manager and ensure sufficient resources and budget throughout

project team The group of people responsible for completion of project activities in order to achieve its goal

protection A means of ensuring that the new idea is not immediately stolen and used by competitors. This can sometime be achieved through legal protection such as patents and trademarks

prototype A model of the final solution that can be tested in order to de-risk the final idea

qualitative market research A structured approach to conducting market research, working with consumers (individually or in groups) to ascertain their needs. This helps those in the marketing and product development teams to understand why consumers buy certain products and services

quality assurance/compliance The function in a business responsible for monitoring new ideas to ensure they comply with agreed standards

quality function deployment (QFD)
A structured approach for linking the needs of the market (musts and wants) with the development of a new idea (features/attributes)

quantitative market research
Consumer research conducted through surveys in order to identify needs for different groups or segments in the market. In order for the results to be valid, the group size needs to be large and representative of the larger population

rapid application development (RAD) A process for developing new products (initially based on software applications) that is fast. In order to achieve rapid speed-to-market, the process adopted will often have activities conducted by different people simultaneously

resource matrix A two-dimensional grid that shows which people (or other resources such as facilities, equipment, material and budgets) will be required on which projects and when

responsibility matrix A two-dimensional grid that shows which members of a project team are involved in which activities

return on innovation investment (ROII) A standard measure of the financial rewards associated with an idea as a ratio of the investment required to make it happen

return on investment (ROI) A standard measure of the financial rewards associated with a project as a ratio of the investment required to make it happen

risk A potential problem associated with a new idea that could occur in the future. Each risk should be identified and quantified in terms of probability and impact, before agreeing what mitigating actions will be taken by whom and when

risk management The process of mitigating the impact of identified risks. Actions will be preventive (proactive action taken to prevent the risk occurring) or contingent (reactive action taken to minimise the impact if it does occur)

roadmapping A graphical representation of future intentions to introduce new ideas, technology or projects

satisfaction surveys A structured process for capturing feedback from customers in order to identify their overall level of satisfaction with the product or service that has been provided. Unfortunately, these surveys are often not a good predictor of future intentions to purchase

scanning A systematic approach to analysing the industry and market in order to identify opportunities for new ideas. The results should feed into forums for innovation and review

scenario planning A process of identifying and evaluativing alternative future states. Future scenarios are identified by looking at future trends or possible discontinuities in the market

screening The process of evaluating a new idea against a series of criteria (see also *V-SAFE*) in order to make a Go, No Go, Modify or Wait decision

search and development (S&D) A phrase reflecting the fact that much innovation comes from searching the internet for good ideas, learning from others and then replicating or replacing rather than starting from scratch

segmentation The process of dividing a large market into smaller groups. Each sub-group will have similar characteristics and will therefore simplify the process of analysis and targeting

sensitivity analysis An assessment of the impact of changing a single variable on the overall performance or result of introducing a new idea

specification A detailed description of the features and performance impact associated with a new idea

stage A phase in the development and commercialisation of a new idea with clear deliverables and outputs. A Go/No Go decision will typically be made at the end of each phase

stage-gate process A structured process used to develop and commercialise new ideas. Each stage will have clear outputs or deliverables

strategic partnering An alliance or partnership between two organisations to improve their operational processes, create new products or exploit new markets

strategy The future vision – it identifies the basis on which an organisation or team will compete or differentiate itself, its products and services to its chosen target markets and customers

suggestion scheme A process by which new ideas identified by employees are captured, sorted and fed into a forum for future evaluation. This process is increasingly managed through websites

supply chain A group of companies involved in the supply of products and services to consumers, where each company will be a supplier to one of the others

SWAG A sophisticated wide-arsed guess

SWOT analysis An assessment of an idea, product or market using four criteria: strengths, weaknesses, opportunities and threats

target market The group of customers or consumers that are most likely to buy the product, or that represent the most significant strategic potential

team leader The person ultimately responsible for the performance of the team and for managing and motivating team members

technology roadmap A top-level plan or graphic that shows how technology will evolve over future periods and how it will impact the evolution of products and processes

technology transfer The process of transferring expertise, knowledge and intellectual property (IP) from one organisation to another

test market A market of limited scope used to test a new idea. It needs to be small enough to mitigate the risk of failure, but it also needs to reflect the target market so that results will guide implementation

think tank A group or environment set up specifically to generate and evaluate new ideas. It will often be very distinct from typical operations in order to identify more creative and distinctive solutions

thinking hats A term developed by Edward de Bono to reflect the differing roles that people can fulfil during a meeting or workshop. This approach can be a stimulus for creative thinking

time to market The time taken to develop a new idea from concept to implementation or initial sales in the market. For some organisations, a faster time to market will provide a source of advantage

total quality management (TQM) A methodology and associated toolset used for the continuous improvement of a team or process

trademarks Registered brands or logos that prohibit others from copying or mimicking the design

unique selling proposition (USP) A distinctive set of features and benefits that provide a competitive advantage in the market. The USP can only be identified through a detailed understanding of customer musts and wants, and of competitor performance

user Any person who uses a product or a service. As the consumer, they will gain the benefit but they will not necessarily be the buyer

value chain As an idea or product moves through each stage of its development from idea to implementation, value is added. The value chain identifies each step and relative value added

value proposition A simple statement that describes the value a product or service gives to the customer or consumer. The word value implies that it will describe benefits (possibly measured in financial terms) and not features or attributes

value-added The result of adding or combining features to a product or service in order to increase the overall worth

virtual team A team working towards a common purpose but not located in the same facility or working for the same boss. Through the use of technology, this team may not come together at all

vision A view of the future state of the business: what it could be if everything went according to plan

voice of the customer (VOC) An understanding of the musts and wants of different customer or consumer groups and the relevance to the organisation and individual teams

V-SAFE Generic criteria used to screen and prioritise new ideas:

V = value to the organisation in terms of financial impact;

S = suitable, given the current situation and strategy;

A = acceptable to the differing stakeholders impacted;

F = feasible, given current resource and budget constraints; and

E = enduring beyond the current time period

whiteboard A board for capturing ideas, secured to the wall of a corridor or work room in order to allow ideas for performance improvement to be captured

window of opportunity The period of time during which a new idea or product can be launched successfully

workplan A detailed plan identifying the tasks required to successfully implement an idea, together with ownership and timings

INDEX

Page numbers in **bold** relate to entries in the Glossary.

3 Ts 125
5 forces **194**
6 hats 130
6 Ps xvii–xix, 33

ABP *see* annual business planning
acceptability 44–6
accessibility of information 169
actioning ideas 180
active support 22
ad hoc day-to-day activities 40–1
adoption curves **190**
advertising innovations 84
advertising materials 185
advertorials 144
aesthetics, products 153
alliances **190**
alpha tests **190**
alternative business models 78
alternatives 175–6
analyses **190**
　competitors 161, **191**
　critical path 87
　customer value **191**
　gap **192**
　market 182
　qualitative 183
　risk 84
　root cause 21
　sensitivity **196**
　SWOT *see* SWOT analyses
Animalcare Group 180
annual business planning (ABP) 39, 40, 80
annual cycles 86
antecedents 121–3
Apple 153
asking 'so what?' 86, 173
asking 'why?' 81
attitudes 19, 21, 116
attributes 116–17
　testing **190**

audits 184
　innovation *see* innovation
　internal 182
　performance 186
authorisations 185
awareness 1–3, **190**
　innovation audits 17–27
　innovation in a nutshell 5–15

B2B (business-to-business) **190**
B2C (business-to-consumer) **191**
bad ideas, filtering out 12
balanced scorecards **190**
balanced teams 88
barriers 82, 109, 132–4
behaviours 19, 22, 88, 116, 121–3
benchmarking 145, 179, **190**
benefits **190**
　communicating 134
　tangible 43–4
bespoke services 90–1
best ideas, sources 12
best practice 89, 161, 186, **190**
beta tests **190**
beyond NPD **190**
Birchall, David 59, 90–2
Birkinshaw, Julian 25–7
blame cultures 54
blame-free cultures 125
blogs 74
board work 143
BOC-Linde 100
boring 131
bottom-line performance 54–5
boundaries 9, 105, 111, 119
BP 180
brainstorming 9, 39, 42, 130, 182, **190**
brands 183, **190**
breaks, taking 105–6
breakthrough thinking 21, 82
breakthroughs 54, 107, 160, 182, **190**
briefs 183, 184

Bruce, A. 167
budgets
   allocation 13, 47
   availability 102
   feasibility and 45
   ideas generation 160
   information 111
   internal ideas markets 41
   projects 161, 185
   requirements 85
   sufficiency 88
building better organisations 25–7
building teams 128–34
Burns, T. 14–15
business-as-usual 88
business cases 47, 183–4, 185, **190**
business contexts 110
business cycles 11
business drivers 20
business environment monitoring 7
business fast track 29–32
   change, implementing 79–92
   fast track top ten 33–60, 105
   technologies 61–78
business imperatives 104
business innovation 11
business needs clarification and
      communication 36
business performance 37, 56
business priorities 36
business snapshots 102
business strategies 110, 117
business-to-business (B2B) **190**
business-to-consumer (B2C) **191**
buzz, creating a 41

cannibalisation **191**
capabilities 37–8, 59–60, 129–30, 146,
      183, 185
capital expenditure (CapEx) 55, 184
capturing return on innovation 58–60
career development 187
career fast track 93–5
   changing roles
      critical time 97–8
      potential pitfalls 98
      worst-case scenario 98–9
   checklist of information requirements
      110–11
   first ten weeks

actions before start 99–100
business snapshots 102
conducting first event 107–8
quick wins 104
reflecting and learning 108–9
reputation building 106–7
stakeholders, getting to know
   101–2
taking breaks 105–6
team SWOTs 103
two-year plans development 109
vision creation 104–5
getting to the top 139
   directors, becoming 147–50
   exit strategy planning 150–1
   focusing on performance 139–41
   inviting challenges 142–7
   keeping up to date 144–6
   methods and qualities required
      149–50
   promotion 146
leadership
   changing oneself 115–21
   coaching 120
   motivating individuals 121–3
   personal attributes 116–17
   physical environments 127–8
   right environment, creating 124–8
   self-perception 115–16
   styles 117–20
   team building 128–34
CBP (core benefit proposition) **191**
central databases 160
challenges
   constructive 111
   creative 124–5
   external 18
   inviting 142–7
   positive 22
champions xix, 18, 49, 51–2, 79, 107,
      162, **191**
change
   barriers to 132–4
   changing oneself 115–21
   implementing
      critical success factors 88–9
      ensuring success – keeping plans
         on track 85–8
      introducing changes 82–5
      planning way ahead 79–82

legal and regulatory 173
political 41, 171
strategic 37–8
supply chains 185
charisma, products 153
charters, projects 182
checklists
    career fast track information
        requirements 110–11
    innovation projects 181–6
    team innovation audits 159–64
Chesborough, Henry 76–7
chief executives 8, 51, 53
close-down reviews 186
coaching 120
Coca-Cola 81–2
coffee breaks 36
collaborate leadership style 118, 119,
    120
command leadership style 117, 118,
    119
commercial exploitation of ideas 5
commercial production 186
commercialisation **191**
commitment 22, 35, 88, 118–19, 134,
    184
commodisation 59
common innovation language 89
common tool sets 162
communication 36
    benefits 134
    internal 54
    plans 101, 184, 185, 186
    strategies 184, 185
    of successes 89
communicative values, products 153
communities of practice 144
competencies 19, 21, 113, 116
competition 90
competitive intelligence **191**
competitiveness 6–7, 146
competitors 143
    analyses 161, **191**
    knowledge of 20, 80
    needs 174–5
    performance 41
    scanning 173–6
    understanding of 20
compliance 184
concepts 183, **191**

concurrent engineering **191**
conferences 84, 144
conflicts of interest, directors 149
congratulations to teams 186
consensus leadership style 117, 118,
    120
consequences 121–3
consistency 165
consolidation strategies 38
constructive challenges 111
consult leadership style 118, 120
consumers **191**
    expectations 7
    feedback 184
    qualitative tests 183
    quantitative tests 184
    validation 183
    See also customers
contingency plans **191**
continuous improvement 7, 11, 108, 165
control 162, 165, 186
convergent thinking **191**
core benefit proposition (CBP) **191**
corporate culture **191**
corporate governance 149
corporate social responsibilities (CSR)
    149
Corven Innovation Cube 100
costs
    life-cycle **193**
    measurement 13
    opportunity **194**
    products 153
    seeking information 145–6
CPA (critical path analysis) 87
creating a buzz 41
creative challenges 124–5
creative culture 18, 53–4
creative ideas 183
creative talents 87–8
creative thinking 21
creative tools 182
creativity 11, **191**
    software 70
    techniques 177–80
credibility 146
crises 38
critical assumptions **191**
critical path analysis (CPA) 87
critical success factors (CSF) 88–9, 102,
    191

critical time for changing roles 97–8
crossing the chasm **191**
CSF *see* critical success factors
CSR (corporate social responsibilities)
149
culture 162
corporate **191**
creative 18, 53–4
definition 53
teams 124–7
See also learning: cultures
current commitments 111
current situation performance
snapshots 140–1
custom-built services solutions to
complex problems 92
customers
base changes 108
concept innovation 91
day-in-the-life-of (DILO) studies 178
expectations 7, 41
feedback 47
focus 160
ideals 178–9
information about 20, 110
insight scanning for using internet
67–8
knowledge of 20
market and customer insight (MCI)
39, 40
meaning **191**
needs 142, 174, **191**
problems 42
purchasing decisions 90
strategic focus 37–8
total customer experience 91
trends 161
value analyses **191**
voice of the customer **198**
See also consumers
customisation 91

Dankbaar, Ben 14–15, 112–13
dashboards 74–5, **191–2**
data capture 169
databases 68–9, 75, 109, 140, 160
day-in-the-life-of (DILO) studies 178
day-to-day activities 40, 87
de Bono, Edward 130
deadlines 104

decision trees **192**
defensive innovation **192**
denial, resistance, exploration,
commitment (DREC) change
model 132–4
dependencies 183
design innovation 152–3
design of experiments (DOE) **192**
design thinking 153
designing innovative organisations
14–15
desire 146
determination 22
development **192**
careers 187
concepts 183
discontinuing 113
ideas 182
stage of projects 47
teams 130–2
workplans 184–5
See also research and development;
search and development
differentiation 7, 58–9, 60, **192**
difficulties 8–10
digital dashboards 74–5, **191–2**
DILO (day-in-the-life-of) studies 178
direction of innovation 160
directors, becoming 147–50
director's toolkit 155–86
disbandment of teams 186
disconnects 180
discontinuities 170–1, 172, **192**
discontinuous innovation **192**
distribution capabilities 185
divergent thinking **192**
diversification strategies 38
DOE (design of experiments) **192**
Downer EDi Mining 22–3
DREC (denial, resistance, exploration,
commitment) change model
132–4
drivers of business 20

early adopters **192**
early indicators 186
ecological performance, products 153
economic movements 41
economic trends 171
economic value added (EVA) **192**

economical costs, products 153
effective prioritisation 161
effectiveness 3, 6–7, 23–4, 54, 55
efficiency 6–7, 41, 55
electronic suggestion schemes 50, 68,
    83, 86
emails 73, 84
emotions 130
encouragement 22
end-to-end processes 161
enduring value 45–6
engineering consultancies 92
entrepreneurs **192**
environmental costs, products 153
environmental trends 41, 172–3
ergonomics 153
ethics 126
EVA (economic value added) **192**
evaluation 130
    of ideas 18, 161
    of progress and performance 89
events 107–8, 111
evidence 103, 130
exhibitions 144
exit stage of projects 47
exit strategies 150–1, **192**
exit workplans 186
expectations, customers 7, 41
experience 88, 105, 122
exploration 133–4
extent of innovation 55, 160
external challenges 18
external contributors 52
external sources of ideas 161
external studies 143

facilitators 9, 36
facts 130
fad, innovation as 10, 14
failure 141, 162
Fast-Track-Me.com 145
feasibility 45–6
features 153, **192**
feedback 47, 183, 184
final specifications 184
financial benefits 109
financial forecasts 183
financial payback 184
financial plans 185
financial screening 183

financials
    initial 183
    products 184
First Direct 174
first to market **192**
five forces **194**
FIW *see* focused innovation workshops
flexibility 13, 87–8, 128–9
focus groups **192**
focus, strategic *see* strategic focus
focused innovation workshops (FIW)
    39–40, 50, 107, 127
forecasts 183, 184, 185
forming 131
forming to mourning model 130–2
forums 74
founders 8
full visibility and control 162
functional specialists 107
functional values, products 153
funding 10, 12, 45
fusion, technology 78
future performance snapshots 141
future workloads 111

Gantt charts 83–4, **192**
gaps 43, 105, 187
    analyses **192**
Gassman, O. 77
gate documents 184, 185
gate keepers **192**
gates **192**
gating 161–2
generation of ideas *see* ideas
global sourcing and innovation 112–13
globalisation 7, 77
Go/No Go decisions 119
Go/No Go (kill)/Modify decisions 48
Go/No Go/Wait decisions 66
go-live activities 184
go-live plans 185
go to market stage of projects 47
goals 13, 128, 161
    See also objectives; targets
Gotzsch, Josiena 152–3
governance 54
    corporate 149
great teams, attributes 128–30
growth options 185

guidance, lack of 9
gut feeling 46, 130

Hamel, Gary 7
handover 151, 186
Happy Computers 25–7
Hicks, D. 135
high value opportunities 88
historic performance snapshots 140

ideals, customers 178–9
ideas **192–3**
　actioning 180
　approval 183
　bad, filtering out 12
　best, sources 12
　commercial exploitation of 5
　converting into action 46
　creative 183
　databases 109
　development 182
　evaluation 18, 161
　generation 39, 89
　　workshops 182
　implementation 181
　internal markets 41
　management not open to 8
　mix of 55
　new 43
　number of 55
　open to 22
　pipelines 68–9
　　evaluation 43–6
　prioritising 43, 180
　reactive 39, 40
　refinement 182
　rewards for, lack of 8–9
　screening 43, 180
　sharing 142
　sources 12
　　external 42–3, 161
　　internal 18, 38–41, 160
　trackers 50
　visibility across businesses 12
ideation 182, **193**
impact 104, 183
implementation 18, 32
　change *see* change
　of ideas 181
　inability of 10

support 184
importance of innovation 5–7, 11
improvement
　continuous *see* continuous
　　improvement
　performance 187
incentives 185, 186
incremental innovations 91, **193**
indicators, early 186
industry advisers 143
industry, knowledge of 20
industry leaders 40, 179–80
information
　accessibility 169
　flows 84
　intensity 90–1
　internet 67–8, 144
　requirements 170
　　career fast track checklist 110–11
　reliability 145
　seeking, cost of 145–6
　validity 145
　See also knowledge
information technology (IT) *see*
　　technologies
initial financials 183
initial meetings 101
initiation
　stage of projects 47
　teams 183
　workplans 182–3
innovation
　audits 17
　　learning 23–4
　　self assessment 19–23
　　of teams 17–19, 108, 159–64
　difficulties 8–10
　importance 5–7, 11
　meaning 5, 11, **193**
　review boards **193**
　strategies **193**
innovation capability 59
innovation executives 160
innovation fatigue 14
innovation overload 43
innovation primers 11
innovation trackers 50
innovation war rooms 39
inquisitive mindsets 21
insight 144, **193**

integrated approach 160
integrated innovation framework 79,
        165–8
integrated product development (IPD)
        193
integration, supply chains 41
intellectual property (IP) 91, **193**
intensity
    information 90–1
    technology 77
internal audits 182
internal communications 54
internal ideas markets 41
internal pilots 47
internal sources of ideas 18, 38–41, 160
internal working parties 143
internet 12
    information sources 67–8, 144
    scanning for market and customer
        insight using 67–8
    social networking 74
    trends 172
intranets 12
intrapreneurs **193**
intuition 46
inversion 179, **193**
involvement 11, 82
IP (intellectual property) 91, **193**
IPD (integrated product development)
        193
ISO-9000 **193**
issues 86, 162
IT (information technology) *see*
        technologies

journals 144
'just do it' (JDI) 81

kaizen **193**
keeping up to date 144–6
key opinion leaders 111
key performance indicators (KPI) 13, 44,
        54–6, 109, 139, 141, 163, 185,
        186
key success factors (KSF) 185
knowledge 122
    of competitors 20, 80
    importance 169–70
    leadership requirements 116
    leveraging 78

new, sourcing for strategy making
        135–7
    self assessment 19, 20
    sources 144
    things to know 42
    See also information
knowledge-based services 92
KPI *see* key performance indicators
KSF (key success factors) 185

lateral thinking 130
launch plans 47, 185
leaders
    enthusiastic 128
    industry 40, 179–80
    information requirements about
        teams 110
    projects **195**
    staying ahead as 187–8
    strong 128
    See also teams: leaders
leadership 3, 18, 115
    attitudes 116
    behaviours 116
    career fast track *see* career fast track
    competencies 116
    effectiveness 23–4
    knowledge requirements 116
    planning 35–7, 160
    self-assessments 116–17
    styles 87, 117–20
    SWOT 117
learning 108–9, 163
    capturing return on innovation 58–60
    cultures 55–6, 162, 165
    innovation audits 23–4
    organisational 59–60
learning organisations 126–7, **193**
legal announcements 41
legal changes 173
legal clearance 184
lessons learned 186
    databases 75, 140
leveraging knowledge 78
life-cycle costs **193**
lifestyle 105
lock-in 91
logistics 9, 185
logistics companies 90
long-term success 11

Macphie 34–5
management
    not open to ideas 8
    of performance *see* performance
    of projects *see* projects
    of risks *see* risks
management consultancies 92
management development courses 143
managers
    cascades 160
    projects **195**
manufacturing 184
    impacts 183
    outsourcing 113
market analyses 182
market and customer insight (MCI) 39,
        40
market development 37–8, **193**
market innovation 11
market research **193**
    qualitative **195**
    quantitative **196**
market scanning 170–3
market share 183, **193**
market testing **193**
market trends 161
marketing 186, **193**
marketing materials 185, 186
markets **194**
    insight scanning for using internet
        67–8
    knowledge of 20
    strategic focus 37–8
Marks & Spencer 180
Martin, B. 135
maturity **194**
maximising potential of teams 17–19
MCI (market and customer insight) 39,
        40
measurement of performance 56
media launch 186
media strategies 185
meetings
    initial 101
    review 86, 106
methods 9
metrics **194**
milestones 83–4
mistakes 12, 19, 53

mix, quantitative tests of 184
mobile phone companies 90
mobile telephony 172
monitoring 186
    business environment 7
    effectiveness 54
    performance 86, 87
Moore, Geoffrey A. 58–60, 99
motivation 121–3, 186
mourning 131

NBD *see* new business development
    needs
        competitors 174–5
        customers *see* customers
negative focus 130
nemawashi **194**
net present values (NPV) **194**
networking 124, 144
neutralisation 58–9, 60
new business development (NBD) 37–8,
        100, **194**
new capabilities 37–8
new ideas 43
new product development (NPD) 36,
        91, **194**
new service development (NSD) 91,
        194
newsletters 84
next job 116
NGT (nominal group technique) **194**
Nokia 6, 126
nominal group technique (NGT) **194**
non-value-added activities 102
norming 131
NPD *see* new product development
NPV (net present values) **194**
NSD (new service development) 91,
        194

objectives 13, 82–3, 110, 129
    See also goals; targets
objects 177–8
offensive innovation **194**
office politics 45
offshoring 113
open innovation (OI) 42–3, 76–8
open-mindedness 13
operating principles 129
operational expenditure (OpEx) 55

operational handover 186
operational impacts 183
operational innovations 36–7
operational priorities 13
operations 166
OpEx (operational expenditure) 55
opinion leaders 111
opportunities 103
  assessments 183
  high value 88
  windows of opportunity 104, **198**
opportunity costs **194**
organisational learning 59–60
outsourcing 112–13
ownership 83, 162

P&L (profit and loss) forecasts 184, 185
Pareto profile **194**
partnering, strategic **197**
partners 143, 180
partnerships
  with complementary organisations
    42–3
past performance snapshots 140
patents **194**
Pavitt, K. 135
payback 184
PDCA (plan-do-check-act) 53, 85–6
PDP (personal development plans) 105,
    186
peer assist 48, **194**
people xviii–xix, 34
  creative culture 53–4
  culture 162
  investment in 36
  managing 85–6
  virtual teams 52
  See also champions
performance xix
  audits 186
  bottom-line 54–5
  business 37, 56
  competitors 41
  current situation snapshots 140–1
  evaluation 89
  focusing on 139–41
  future snapshots 141
  gaps 43
  historic snapshots 140
  improvement 187

indicators 13, **194**
  See also key performance
    indicators
  management 18, 54–7, 85–6, 163
  in market 186
  measurement 56
  monitoring 86, 87
  past snapshots 140
  predictive snapshots 141
  present snapshots 140–1
  products 153
  recognition 162
  reviews 108, 111, 186
  rewards 162
performing 131
personal attributes 116–17
personal development 122
personal development plans (PDP) 105,
    186
personal planning 107
personalised products and services 92
personalities 136
PESTEL 171–3
Peters, Tom 39
physical environments 127–8
pilot launches 185
pilots, internal 47
pipelines xviii, 34, **194**
  ideas 68–9
    evaluation 43–6
    external sources 42–3, 161
    internal sources 38–41, 160
  open innovation 42–3
  scanning 41–2
plan-do-check-act (PDCA) 53, 85–6
planning xviii
  business cycles incorporating
    innovation 11
  change 79–82
  events 107
  exit strategies 150–1
  leadership 35–7, 160
  monitoring 87
  personal 107
  scenario planning **196**
  strategic 86
  strategic focus 37–8, 160
  succession 151
  See also annual business planning;
    plans

plans
  communication *see* communication
  contingency **191**
  financial 185
  go-live 185
  keeping on track 85–8
  launch 185
  managing 85–6
  personal development 105, 186
  projects 184, **195**
  teams 105
  two-year 109
  See also planning; workplans
platforms xviii, 34
  support systems 49–51, 162
PLM (product life-cycle management)
  195
political changes 41, 171
Porter's five forces **194**
portfolios 56, **194**
  assessments 183
  management 48–9
  maps **194–5**
  projects **195**
  See also project and portfolio
    management
positioning 183
positive approach 21
positive challenges 22
positive focus 130
post-launch sales support 186
potential pitfalls of changing roles 98
potential problems 109, 111
potential, quantitative tests of 184
power versus support matrices 101–2
Powergrind 147, 174
PPM *see* project and portfolio
  management
predictive performance snapshots 141
preliminary screening 183
pre-prototypes 183
present performance snapshots 140–1
press releases 185
priorities 10
  business 36
  operational 13
  setting 86
  strategic 160, 182
prioritisation
  effective 161

ideas 43, 180
problems, potential 109, 111
procedures 136
process champions **195**
process maps **195**
process re-engineering **195**
process–system links 65–6
processes xviii, 11, 34
  audits 184
  ideas evaluation 43–6, 161
  improvement 37–8
  innovation programme and portfolio
    management 48–9
  optimisation 184
  project and portfolio management
    46–9
  projects and gating 161–2
production 185, 186
products
  audits 184
  briefs 183, 184
  charisma 153
  communicative values 153
  development 37–8, **195**
    integrated **193**
    See also new product development
  financials 184
  functional values 153
  innovation 11, 52
  life-cycles
    management (PLM) **195**
    meaning **195**
  lines **195**
  meaning **195**
  personalised 92
  refinement 184
  strategic focus 37–8
  understanding of 20
professional bodies 107, 143, 145
professionalism, directors 149
profit and loss (P&L) forecasts 184, 185
profitability 13, 104
progress evaluation 89
progress reviews 108
project and portfolio management
  (PPM) 46–9, 50
  software 71–2
projects 18, 161–2
  charters 182
  checklist 181–6

leaders **195**
management 7, 89, **195**
  competencies 21
  tools and techniques 13
  See also project and portfolio
    management
managers **195**
meaning **195**
plans 184, **195**
portfolios **195**
sponsors **195**
stages 47
teams **195**
promotion 146
proof of concept 183
protection **195**
prototypes 47, 184, **195**
public enquiries 143
public sector 12
public speaking 143
purchasing decisions, customers 90
purpose, shared 128

QFD (quality function development) **196**
qualitative analyses 183
qualitative market research **195**
qualitative tests 183
quality
  assurance **195**
  clearance 184
  compliance **195**
  function development (QFD) **196**
  leadership 118–19
  reviews 184
  total quality management **197**
quantitative market research **196**
quantitative tests 184
question leadership style 118, 119
quick wins 89, 104, 107
quiet areas 36

R&D *see* research and development
rapid application development (RAD)
  196
rational thinking 87–8
reactive ideas 39, 40
recognition 53–4, 162
refinement of ideas 182
reflection 108–9, 187
regulatory announcements 41

regulatory changes 173
regulatory clearance 184
relationships 136, 146
reliability of information 145
reports 84
reputation building 106–7
research and development (R&D) 42,
  77–8, 92
research and technology development
  (RTD) 77
resistance 133
resources
  allocation 47
  availability 102
  feasibility and 45
  financial 10
  individuals 122
  information 111
  matrices **196**
  projects 161
  requirements 83, 85
  sufficiency 88
  technology and 63
respect 129
responsibilities
  directors 148–9
  matrices **196**
  shared 129
return on innovation investment (ROII)
  13, 47, 55, 109, 183, 184, **196**
return on investment (ROI) 13, **196**
review bodies 143
reviews 163
  close-down 186
  meetings 86, 106
  performance *see* performance
  points 83
  process 111
  quality 184
  stakeholders 186
  supply chains 186
rewards 8–9, 53–4, 89, 122–3, 162
Richmond Foods 126, 179–81
rising stars 40
risks 141, **196**
  analyses 84
  assessments 47, 183, 184, 185
  management 21, 141, 162, **196**
  of not being innovative 13
  tolerance to 37

roadmapping 105, **196**
ROI (return on investment) 13, **196**
ROII *see* return on innovation
    investment
roles 110, 162
    changing *see* career fast track:
        changing roles
    directors 148
    teams 129–30
root cause analyses 21
route to market 183, 184
routines 86
RTD (research and technology
    development) 77

S&D *see* search and development
sacred cows 8
sales 186
    forecasts 183
    materials 185
    presentations 185
    teams 80–1, 108
Salter, A. 135
samples 185
satisfaction surveys **196**
Saudi Tourism Commission 120–1
scale (go to market)
    stage of projects 47
    workplans 186
scanning 41–2, 67–8, 161, 170–6, **196**
scenario planning **196**
scope 111
scope creep 83
screening 43, 180, 183, **196**
search and development (S&D) 42–3,
    125–6, 170, **196**
segmentation **196**
self-assessments
    innovation audits 19–23
    leadership 116–17
self-development 143
self-perception 115–16
senior management 10, 35, 36, 82, 88
Senker, J. 135
sensitivity analyses **196**
services
    bespoke 90–1
    custom-built solutions to complex
        problems 92
    information intensity 90–1

innovation 11, 90–2
    knowledge-based 92
    new service development 91, **194**
    personalised 92
    standardised 90–1
    strategic focus 37–8
    understanding of 20
services companies 12
shared purpose 128
shared responsibilities 129
shared values 129
sharing ideas 142
Sharp, M. 135
Shell 180
SIG (special interest groups) 74
sign-offs 185
six hats 130
six Ps xvii–xix, 33
skills 13, 162
    audits 184
    development 89, 105, 122
    existing 52
    requirements 52
    self assessment 19
    teams 88, 129–30
skunk works 39
SMART 141
smart phones 83
'so what?' test 86, 173
social costs, products 153
social networking software 74
social trends 171–2
Soderquist, Klas Eric 76–8
software
    creativity 70
    social networking 74
solution briefs 183
special interest groups (SIG) 74
specifications 47, 184, **197**
sponsors, projects **195**
stage-gate processes **197**
stages 47–8, **197**
stakeholders 110
    buy-in 184
    commitment 184
    communicating to 84
    getting to know 101–2
    involvement 82
    reviews 186
Stalker, G.M. 14–15

standardised services 90–1
statutory responsibilities, directors
        148–9
staying ahead as leaders 187–8
Steliaros, Rebecca 135–7
Stewart, Henry 25–7
storming 131
strategic change 37–8
strategic focus 18, 37–8, 160
strategic partnering **197**
strategic planning 86
strategic priorities 160, 182
strategies 166, **197**
    innovation fit with 55
    making, sourcing new knowledge for
        135–7
    teams 105
strengths 103
structured focused innovation
        workshops 39–40
structures 9
substitutes 175–6
success
    communication of 89
    critical success factors *see* critical
        success factors
    ensuring 85–8
    hurdles 185
    increasing changes of 88–9
    indicators 185
    long-term 11
    rates 56
succession planning 151
suggestion schemes 12, 50, 55, 68, 83,
        86, **197**
suitability 44
suppliers 47, 110, 170
supply chains 143, 184, 186, **197**
    audits 184
    changes 185
    impacts on 183
    mapping 47
    opportunities for integration or
        efficiency 41
    reviews 186
support 184
    active 22
    cultures 162
    post-launch sales 186
    systems 18, 49–51, 162

visible 22
support versus power matrices 101–2
supportiveness 129
surveys, satisfaction **196**
SWAG 145–6, 169, **197**
SWOT analyses 111, **197**
    leadership 117
    teams 103
synergy 21, 183
systems audits 184

talents, creative 87–8
tangible benefits 43–4
targets
    audiences 183
    markets **197**
    time 82–3
    See also goals; objectives
teams
    assessments 17–19
    balanced 88
    behaviours 121–3
    building 128–34
    capabilities 129–30
    champions 51
    coaching 120
    congratulations 186
    culture 124–7
    development 130–2
    disbandment 186
    effectiveness 3, 23–4
    email communications 73
    flexibility 128–9
    goals 128
    great, attributes 128–30
    initiation 183
    innovation audits 17–19, 108, 159–64
    issues 129
    leaders 8, **197**
        strong and enthusiastic 128
    leaders' information requirements
        about 110
    maximising potential 17–19
    motivation 121–3, 186
    objectives 110, 129
    operating principles 129
    plans 105
    projects **195**
    respect 129
    roles 129–30

teams (*continued*)
    sales 80–1, 108
    shared purpose 128
    shared responsibilities 129
    shared values 129
    sharing ideas with other internal
        teams 142
    skills 129–30
    strategies 105
    supportiveness 129
    SWOTs 103
    trust 129
    virtual *see* virtual teams
technical performance, products 153
technical tests 184
techniques *see* tools and techniques
technologies 32, 49, 57, 61
    activities to focus on 63–5
    advancements 41
    awareness of 66
    considering 61–3
    discontinuities 172
    fusion 78
    getting started 61–5
    intensity 77
    keeping balance 75–6
    process–system links 65–6
    tools supporting sustainable
        approach to innovation 66–75
    top 66–76
    use 65–6
    See also software
technology-led innovation 92
technology roadmaps **197**
technology transfers **197**
ten minutes out each day 99
tenacity 13
terrorists 125
Tesco 180
test markets **197**
tests 184
themed focused innovation workshops
    39–40
things to know 42
think tanks **197**
thinking
    breakthrough 21, 82
    convergent **191**
    creative 21
    design thinking 153

    divergent **192**
    inversion 179
    lateral 130
    rational 87–8
thinking hats 130, **197**
threats 103
three Ts 125
time 45, 63–5, 160
    constraints 9
    ideas generation 160
    leadership styles and 117–18
    targets 82–3
time to market **197**
timelines 83–4
timetables 185
timing 83, 183
to-do lists 99, 108
tolerance to risk 37
tools and techniques 31
    common tool sets 162
    competitor scanning 169–76
    creative 182
    creativity techniques 177–80
    director's toolkit 155–7
    electronic suggestion schemes 50
    innovation trackers 50
    integrated innovation framework
        165–8
    introduction to 33–5
    market scanning 169–76
    people 34, 51–4, 162
    performance 34, 54–7, 163
    pipelines 34, 38–43, 160–1
    planning 33, 35–8, 160
    platforms 34, 49–51, 162
    processes 34, 43–9, 161–2
    project checklist 181–6
    project management 13
top technologies 66–76
top ten innovation elements 33–60, 105
total customer experience 91
total quality management (TQM) **197**
tourists 125
Tovstiga, George 58–60
TQM (total quality management) **197**
trade magazines 144
trademarks 184, **197**
training 52, 183
transformers 125
trends 41, 161, 170, 171–2

trust 129
Tuckman, Bruce Wayne 130
two-year plans development 109

unique features, products 153
unique selling propositions (USP) 102,
182, **197**
Universal DVD 62
universities 135–7
urgency 104
users **197–8**
   feedback 184
   tests 184
   validation 183
USP *see* unique selling propositions
utility companies 90

V-SAFE 43–6, 66, 180, 183, **198**
validation 47, 183, 185
validity of information 145
value 43–6, 63–5, 183
value-added 102, **198**
value chains **198**
value propositions **198**
values, shared 129

video conferencing 72–3
virtual teams 52, 107, **198**
visibility 12, 162, 165
visible support 22
vision 104–5, **198**
voice of the customer (VOC) **198**
von Tunzelmann, N. 135

waste 58
Watkins, Michael 97
weaknesses 103
websites 144
whiteboards 12, **198**
wikis 74
windows of opportunity 104, **198**
work commitments 105
working parties, internal 143
workplans 181–6, **198**
workshops 9, 11, 80, 104, 123, 182, 183
   See also focused innovation
      workshops
worst-case scenario, changing roles
   98–9

ZIBA 152–3

FAST TRACK TO SUCCESS

9780273719908

9780273721789

9780273721802

9780273719885

9780273719922

9780273721765

EVERYTHING YOU NEED TO ACCELERATE YOUR CAREER

FT Prentice Hall

FINANCIAL TIMES